RUBEM ALVES

# WHAT IS RELIGION?

*Translated from the Portuguese
by Don Vinzant*

ORBIS BOOKS

Maryknoll, New York 10545

The Catholic Foreign Mission Society of America (Maryknoll) recruits and trains people for overseas missionary service. Through Orbis Books Maryknoll aims to foster the international dialogue that is essential to mission. The books published, however, reflect the opinions of their authors and are not meant to represent the official position of the society.

Originally published in 1981 as *O que é religião?* Editora Brasiliense S.A., 01042 Rua Barão de Itapetininga, 93, São Paulo, Brazil
Copyright © 1981 by Rubem A. Alves

English translation copyright © 1984 by Orbis Books, Maryknoll, NY 10545

**Library of Congress Cataloging in Publication Data**

Alves, Rubem A., 1933-
  What is religion?

  Translation of: O que é religião?
  Bibliography: p.
  1. Religion. I. Title
BL48.A48513   1984       200        83-19398
ISBN 0-88344-705-3 (pbk.)

# *Contents*

## Bibliography of Works Cited

Berger, Peter L. and Thomas Luckmann. *The Social Construction of Reality: A Treatise in the Sociology of Knowledge.* New York: Doubleday, 1966.

Blake, William. *The Complete Poetry and Prose of William Blake.* Rev. ed. Edited by David V. Erdman. Berkeley and Los Angeles: University of California Press, 1982.

Buber, Martin. *I and Thou.* Translated by Walter Kaufmann. New York: Scribner's, 1970.

Camus, Albert. *The Rebel.* New York: Knopf, 1956.

Carroll, Lewis. *Alice's Adventures in Wonderland.* New York: World, 1946.

Cassirer, Ernst. *An Essay on Man: An Introduction to a Philosophy of Human Culture.* New Haven: Yale University Press, 1944.

Durkheim, Emile (Durkheim a). *The Elementary Forms of the Religious Life.* Translated by Joseph Ward Swain. New York: Free Press, 1965.

—— (Durkheim b). *The Rules of Sociological Method.* Translated by Sarah A. Solovay and John H. Mueller. Edited by George E. G. Catlin. Chicago: University of Chicago Press, 1938.

Feuerbach, Ludwig. *The Essence of Christianity.* Translated by George Eliot. New York: Harper, 1957.

Hume, David. *An Enquiry Concerning Human Understanding.* In *Hume: Selections.* Edited by Charles W. Hendel, Jr. New York: Charles Scribner's Sons, 1927.

Macleish, Archibald. "Ars Poetica." In *The Treasury of American Poetry: A Collection of the Finest by America's Poets.* Selected and with an Introduction by Nancy Sullivan. New York: Doubleday, 1978.

Mannheim, Karl. *Ideology and Utopia: An Introduction to the Sociology of Knowledge.* Translated by Louis Wirth and Edward Shils. New York: Harcourt, 1961.

——(Marx and Engels b). *On Religion.* New York: Schocken, 1964.

Marx, Karl and Friedrich Engels (Marx and Engels a). *The German Ideology.* Rev. ed. Moscow: Progress, 1976.

Nietzsche, Friedrich. *Thus Spoke Zarathustra: A Book for All and None.* Translated by Walter Kaufmann. New York: Viking, 1966.

Orwell, George. *Nineteen Eighty-Four.* New York: Harcourt, 1949.

Otto, Rudolf. *The Idea of the Holy.* New York: Oxford University Press, 1950.

Pascal, Blaise. *Pascal's Pensées.* Translated by Martin Turnell. New York: Harper & Brothers, 1962.

Saint-Exupéry, Antoine de. *The Little Prince.* New York: Harcourt, 1943.

Sartre, Jean-Paul. *The Psychology of Imagination.* New York: Philosophical Library, 1948.

Schleiermacher, Friedrich. *The Christian Faith.* Translated by H. R. McIntosh and J. S. Stewart. Edinburgh: T. & T. Clark, 1948.

Wittgenstein, Ludwig. *Tractatus Logico-Philosophicus.* Atlantic Highlands, N.J.: Humanities Press, 1961.

# CHAPTER ONE

# *Perspectives*

*Here are priests; and though they are my enemies, pass
by them silently and with sleeping swords. . . . My
blood is related to theirs. [Nietzsche: 90-91]*

There was a time when the unbelievers, without either
the love of God or religion, were rare. So rare that they
surprised themselves with their unbelief and hid it, as if it
were a contagious plague. And in fact it was. So much a
plague that many were burned at the stake so that their
shamefulness would not contaminate the innocent. All
were educated to see and hear the things of the religious
world. And daily conversations, this tenuous thread that
sustains world visions, confirmed, by means of miracles,
apparitions, visions, and mystical experiences, divine and
demonic, that this was a marvelous and enchanted universe—a universe in which, behind and through each thing
and each event, a spiritual power was hidden and revealed.
Gregorian chant, the music of Bach, the canvases of
Hieronymus Bosch and Pieter Bruegel, the Gothic cathe-
dral, *The Divine Comedy*—all these works are expressions

Abbreviated citations refer to works listed in the Bibliography. (Where the
reference is to an author two of whose works are listed, the letters *a* or *b* will be
used to indicate whether the citation is from the first or second of the works
listed.)

**1**

of a world that lived its temporal life beneath the lights and shadows of eternity. The physical universe structured itself around the drama of the human soul. And perhaps this is the mark of all religions, however distant they are from each other—*the effort to envision all of reality from a point of departure in the necessity that life make sense.*

But something happened. The spell was broken. The sky, inhabited by God and God's saints, suddenly became empty. Virgins no longer appeared in grottos. Miracles became more rare and began to occur always in distant places to unknown persons. Science and technology advanced triumphantly, constructing a world in which God was not necessary as a working hypothesis. Indeed, one of the marks of scientific knowledge is its rigorous methodological atheism: biology does not invoke evil spirits to explain epidemics, neither do economists invoke the powers of hell to explain inflation, just as modern astronomy, far removed from Kepler, does not seek to hear unusual divine harmonies in the mathematical regularities of the stars.

Did religion disappear? Not at all. It endures, and frequently exhibits a vitality that had been thought extinct. But it cannot be denied that it can no longer go to some of the places that used to belong to it: it has been expelled from the centers of scientific knowledge and from the chambers where the decisions are made that determine lives. Truly, I do not know of a single instance in which the theologians have been summoned to collaborate in setting up military plans. Nor do I have knowledge of the moral sensibilities of the prophets having been utilized for the development of economic programs. It is highly doubtful that any industrial magnate, convinced that nature is God's creation and therefore sacred, has lost sleep over pollution.

The religious experience endures—*outside* the world of science, of factories, of plants, of weapons, of money, of banks, of advertising, of sales, of purchases, of profit. It is understandable that, unlike what occurred in a not very distant past, few parents dream of a priestly career for their sons.

The situation has changed. In the sacred world, the religious experience was an integral part of everyone, in the same way as sex, skin color, the parts of the body, and speech. A person without religion was an anomaly. In the desacralized world, things are inverted. Less among the common people, outside academic circles, but intensely among those who pretend to have passed through a scientific enlightenment, the embarrassment caused by a personal religious experience is unequalled. For obvious reasons: to admit being religious is the equivalent of admitting being an inhabitant of the enchanted and magical world of the past, even if only partially. And the embarrassment grows, the closer we get to the social sciences, the very sciences that study religion.

How is this possible?

How can we explain this distance between knowledge and experience?

It is not difficult. It is not necessary for the scientist to have a personal involvement with amoebas, comets, and poisons in order to understand and know them. This analogy being valid, it may be concluded that it is not necessary for the scientist to have had personal religious experiences as a prerequisite for his or her investigation into religious phenomena.

The problem is whether the analogy can be invoked for all situations. Could a person born deaf comprehend the aesthetic experience that one has upon hearing Beethoven's Ninth Symphony? It seems not. Nevertheless, it would be perfectly possible for him or her to study the science of human behavior derived from the aesthetic experience. The deaf person could go to concerts and without hearing a single musical note observe and rigorously measure the actions which people performed and the things which happened within them, from physiological reactions to patterns of social relationship—consequences of personal aesthetic experiences which the researcher personally could not undergo.

But what would he or she have to say about music? Nothing.

I believe that the same thing occurs with respect to religion. This is the reason why, as an introduction to his classic work on the subject, Rudolf Otto advised those who had never had any religious experience not to continue reading the book (Otto: 8).

And here we would have to ask ourselves if there really exist people in whom religious questions have been radically extirpated. Religion is not liquidated with abstinence from sacramental acts and the absence of sacred places, just as sexual desire is not eliminated with vows of chastity. And it is when pain knocks at the door, and technical resources are exhausted, that there is awakened among people the seers, the exorcists, the magicians, the healers, the "blessers," the priests, the prophets and poets, those who pray and supplicate without knowing for sure to whom. And then it is that the questions arise about the meaning of life and the meaning of death, questions from the times of insomnia and times before the mirror. What frequently occurs is that the same religious questions of the past are again articulated, but clothed now in secular symbols. The names have been metamorphosed. The same religious function persists. Therapeutic promises of individual peace, inner harmony, liberation from anguish, hopes for fraternal and just social orders, for the resolution of conflicts among persons, and for harmony with nature, however disguised they might be with the cosmetics of psychoanalytic/psychological jargon, or with the language of sociology, political science, and economics, will always be expressions of individual and social problems around which religious webs have been woven. If this is true, we shall be forced to conclude not that our world has been secularized, but that gods and religious hopes have gained new names and labels, and that the priests and prophets have gained new clothes, new positions, and new names.

It is easy to identify, isolate, and study religion as the exotic behavior of backward and remote social groups. But it is necessary to recognize it as an invisible presence, subtle, disguised, that constitutes one of the threads with which is woven the happenings of our daily existence. Religion is closer to our personal experience than we wish to admit. The study of religion, therefore, far from being a window that opens only on panoramic vistas, is a mirror in which we see ourselves. Here the science of religion is also the science of ourselves: wisdom, delicious knowledge. As Ludwig Feuerbach poetically said:

Consciousness of God is self-consciousness, knowledge of God is self-knowledge. . . . Religion [is] the solemn unveiling of a man's hidden treasures, the revelation of his intimate thoughts, the open confession of his love-secrets. [Feuerbach: 12–13]

And we can add: What hidden treasure is not religious? And what intimate confession of love is not pregnant with gods? And just who is this person who is empty of hidden treasures and secrets of love?

# CHAPTER TWO

# *Symbols of Absence*

*Man is the only creature who refuses to be what he is.*
*[Camus: 11]*

Through millions of years, animals have survived by
means of physical adaptation. Their sharpened teeth and
claws, their hard skulls and tough shells, their poisons and
odors, their hypersensitive senses, their capacity to run,
jump, and dig, and their strange ability to blend in with
the terrain, the barks of trees, leaves—all these are manifestations of bodies marvelously adapted to the nature
of their surroundings. But the phenomenon is not just
limited to the adaptation of the organism to the environment. The animal makes nature adapt to its body. And
we see the dams constructed by beavers, the hiding-places
of armadillos, the ant-hills, the beehives, and the ovenbird's house. And the extraordinary thing is that all this
wisdom for survival and this artistic ability is transmitted
from generation to generation, silently, without words and
without teachers. I think of the wasp that goes out hunting
for a spider, battles it, stings it, paralyzes it, and drags it
back to her nest. There she deposits her eggs and dies.

Some time later, the larvae will hatch and feed on the fresh meat of the immobile spider. They will grow. And without having been taught or having attended any school, one day they will hear the silent voice of wisdom that has lived in their bodies for thousands of years: "It is time. I must go hunt a spider. . . ."

And what is extraordinary is the time-frame in which animals have had this experience. The mollusk appears to make its shells today in the same way it made them millions of years ago. And as for the ovenbird, I know of no alteration, for better or for worse, that has been introduced into its house-plans. Goldfinches sing today just as they sang in the past, and beaver dams, beehives, and anthills have remained unaltered for century upon century. *Each body keeps producing the same thing.* The animal is its body. Its biological programming is complete, closed, perfect. There are no unsolved problems. And for this very reason, there is no opening at all for anything new to be invented. Animals have no history, practically speaking, as we understand history. Their life is processed in a world structurally closed. The adventure of freedom is not offered them, but neither do they receive, in counterpoint, the curse of neurosis and the terror of anguish.

How very different things are with human beings! If the animal's body allows me to foresee the kinds of things it will produce—the form of its shell, of its burrow, of its nest, the style of its sexual courtship, the music of its sounds—and if the things that the animal produces permit me to know from what kind of body they come, there is nothing similar that can be said of human beings. Here is a newborn child. From the genetic point of view she is already totally determined: skin color, eyes, blood type, sex, susceptibility to disease. But what will her style be like? For what ideals and values will she fight? And what things will come from her hands? And here the geneticists, great though their knowledge be, have to keep silent. For the human being—unlike the animal, who *is* its body—*has* his or her body. It is not the body that makes the person. It is the person who makes the body. To be sure, biological programming has not abandoned us altogether. Little children continue to be begotten and to be born, most of the time perfect, without the fathers and the mothers knowing what is going on there inside the mother's womb. And it is likewise biological programming that controls hormones, blood pressure, heartbeat. The fact of the matter is that biological programming continues to function. But this says little if anything about what we are going to accomplish in the great world out there. The human world, made by work and love, is a blank page about the wisdom that our bodies have inherited from our ancestors.

The fact is that human beings refuse to be what animals are—the sum total of what the past offers them. They have become inventors of worlds. And they have planted gardens, made huts, houses, and palaces, constructed drums, flutes, and harps, written poems, changed their bodies, covering them with paint, metal, brands, and cloth, invented flags, built altars, buried their dead and prepared them for travel, and in their absence sung laments for days and nights.

And when we ask ourselves about the inspiration for these worlds which men and women have imagined and built, we are taken by astonishment. And this is because we discover that here, in contrast to the animal world, where the imperative of survival reigns supreme, the body does not have the last word. People are capable of committing suicide. Or of giving their bodies over to death, as

long as from death another world will be born, as many
revolutionaries have done. Or of abandoning themselves
to a monastic life, in a total renunciation of will, of sex, of
the pleasure of food. To be sure, I may be told that these
are extreme examples, and that the majority of persons do
not commit suicide, or die for a better world, or bury
themselves in a monastery. I have to agree. But on the
other hand, it is necessary to recognize that all of our daily
life is based on a constant check upon the immediate im-
peratives of our body. Sexual impulses, food-likes, nasal
sensibilities, the biological rhythm of waking/sleeping,
have long since stopped being natural expressions of the
body, because the body itself has been transformed from
an entity of nature into a creation of culture. Culture, the
name which has been given to these worlds which men and
women have imagined and constructed, begins only at the
moment when the body ceases to give the orders. This is
the reason why, differently from larvae abandoned by
the mother wasp, children have to be educated. It is necessary for their elders to *teach* them what the world is. There
cannot be culture without education. Everyone who ap-
proaches and speaks with them, tells stories, sings a song,
makes gestures, encourages, applauds, laughs, corrects,
threatens, is a teacher, who is *describing* this invented
world—substituting in this way for the body's innate wisdom, since on the threshold of the human world, this wisdom ceases to speak.

If the body, as a brute biological fact, is neither source
nor model for the creation of cultural worlds, the question
remains, why do human beings create culture? Why do
they abandon the solid and ready-made world of nature in
order to build, spider-like, the webs upon which they live?

Why do they plant gardens? And produce sculptures,
paintings, symphonies, poems?

And the great and the small join hands, and go around in a circle, and fly kites, and dance . . .

. . . And weep for their dead, and weep for themselves in their dead, and build altars, and speak of the ultimate conquest of the body, the final triumph over nature, the immortality of the soul, the resurrection of the flesh.

And I have to confess that I do not know how to answer these questions. I simply note that it is this way. And everything that the human being does reveals to me an anthropological mystery. Animals survive by physical adaptation to the world. We, on the contrary, appear to be constitutionally unadaptable to the world as it is given to us. Our philosophical tradition puts forth its best efforts to demonstrate that we are rational beings, beings of thought. But the cultural productions that come from our hands, to the contrary, suggest that we are beings of *desire*. Desire is a symptom of privation, of absence. One does not have longing for the loved one who is present. Longing appears only at a distance, when we happen to be away from affection. Again, you do not have hunger—the supreme desire for physical survival—on a full stomach. Hunger only appears when the body is deprived of bread. Hunger is the witness of the absence of food. It is always this way with desire. Desire belongs to beings that feel deprived, that do not encounter pleasure in what space and the present moment have to offer. It is understandable that culture would not be the exact duplicate of nature. For what culture seeks to create is precisely the *desired object*. Human activity therefore cannot be understood simply as a battle for survival that, once resolved, can give itself over to the luxury of producing something superfluous. Culture does not arise only where human beings have dominated nature. Dying people stammer out songs, and exiles and prisoners produce poems. Do funeral songs exorcise death? It seems not. But they do exorcise terror, and sound out the groan of protest and the reticence of hope. And captivity poems do not break chains or open doors, but, for reasons we do not well understand, it seems that men and women feed upon them and that, on the tenuous thread of speech that enunciates them, there surges forth anew the voice of protest and the splendor of hope.

The suggestion that comes to us from psychoanalysis is that we make culture in order to create the objects of our desire. The unconscious project of the ego, regardless of time and place, *is to encounter a world that can be loved*. There are situations in which we *can* plant gardens and gather flowers. There are other situations, however, of *impotence*, in which the objects of our love exist only by means of the enchantment of the imagination and the miraculous power of the word. They come together in this way—love, desire, imagination, hands, and symbols—to create a world that makes sense, that can be in harmony with the values of those who have constructed it, that can be a mirror, a friendly space, a home. They can be the concrete realization of the objects of desire or, to make use of terminology that comes from Hegel, they can be an objectification of spirit.

We have, then, to ask ourselves: What culture is it in which this ideal has been fulfilled? In none. It is possible to discern the *intention* of the cultural act, but it appears that its *effective realization* forever escapes what is concretely possible for us. Around the garden is the desert that eventually devours it; the *ordo amoris* (Max Scheler) is surrounded by chaos; and the body that seeks love and pleasure is confronted with rejection, cruelty, loneliness, injustice, prison, torture, pain, and death. Culture appears to suffer from the same weakness that the magical rituals suffered from. We recognize its intention, we take note of

its failure—and there remains only the hope that, some-
how, someday, reality will harmonize with desire. And as
long as desire is not fulfilled, it remains to be sung, told,
celebrated, have poems written about it, symphonies composed about it, and celebrations and festivals proclaimed
about it. And the fulfillment of the intention of culture is
then transferred to the sphere of symbols.

Symbols resemble horizons. Horizons—where do you
find them? The closer we get to them, the more they flee
from us. And, nevertheless, they surround us, behind,
around, before. They are the points of reference for our
journeying. There are always the horizons of night and the
horizons of the early morning. The hopes of the act by
which people have created culture, present in its own
failure, are horizons that indicate directions. This is the
reason why we cannot understand a culture when we re-
strict ourselves to contemplate its technical/practical
triumphs. For it is just at the point where it failed that the
symbol breaks forth, testimony to the things still absent,
longing for the things that have not been born.

And it is here that religion appears, a web of symbols, a
network of desires, a confession of hope, a horizon of
horizons, the most fantastic and pretentious attempt to
transubstantiate nature.

It is not composed of the extraordinary.

There are *things* to be considered: altars, sanctuaries,
food, perfume, palaces, chapels, temples, amulets, collars,
books.

And also *gestures*, like silences, looks, prayers, incantations, renunciations, songs, poems, processions, pilgrim-
ages, exorcisms, miracles, celebrations, feasts, adorations.

And we shall now have to ask ourselves about the special properties of these things and gestures that make them
inhabitants of the *sacred* world, while other things and

other gestures, without aura or power, continue to live in the profane world.

There are properties which, in order to make themselves felt and respected, depend exclusively upon themselves. For example, before human beings existed, the sun already gave heat, rain fell, and plants and animals filled the world. All this would have existed and functioned even if human beings had never existed, had never said a word or made a gesture. And it is probable that it will continue even after our disappearance. For this is a matter of natural realities—separate from the desire, from the will, from the practical activity of men and women. There are also gestures that possess efficacy in themselves. The finger that pulls a trigger, the hand that drops a bomb, the feet that make a bicycle go: even if the man who is shot never knows or hears a single word, even if those who are bombed have never been given any warning, and even if there has been no conversation between the feet and the wheels, it does not matter; the gestures have an efficacy within themselves and are, practically, inhabitants of the world of nature.

No fact, thing, or gesture, however, is found already bearing the marks of the sacred. The sacred is not an inherent efficacy within anything. On the contrary, things and gestures *become* religious when human beings baptize them as such. Religion is born with the power human beings have *to give names to things*, thus making a distinction between things of secondary importance and things on which their destiny, their life, and their death depend. And this is the reason why, making an abstraction of the sentiments and personal experiences which accompany the encounter with the sacred, religion presents us with a certain kind of speech, of discourse, a network of symbols. With these symbols human beings discriminate objects,

times, and spaces, constructing with their help a sacred
canopy, with which they can put a cover upon their world.
Why? Perhaps because without it the world would be too
cold and dark. With our sacred symbols, we exorcise fear
and build dikes against chaos.

And in this way inert things—rocks, plants, springs—
and gestures, common in themselves, come to be the visible signs of an invisible network of meanings, that come to
exist because of the human power to give names to things,
thereby attributing value to them. It was not for nothing
that we referred to religion as "the most fantastic and pretentious attempt to transubstantiate nature." In fact, objects and gestures, in themselves insensitive and indifferent
to human destiny, are magically integrated with it. Camus
observed that it is curious that no one is disposed to die for
scientific truths. What difference does it make if the sun is
going around the earth or if the earth is going around the
sun? The fact is that scientific truths refer to objects of the
most radical and deliberate indifference to life and death,
to the happiness or unhappiness of people. There are
truths that are cold and inert. Our destiny does not depend
upon them. When, on the contrary, we deal with symbols
upon which we depend, our whole body trembles. And this
trembling is the emotional/existential sign of the experience of the sacred.

About what does religious language speak?

Within the limits of the profane world we deal with
things that are concrete and visible. Thus we discuss people, bills, the cost of living, things done by politicians,
national revolutions, and our latest attack of rheumatism.
When we enter the sacred world, however, we discover
that a transformation has occurred. For now language
refers to *invisible things*, things which go beyond our five
senses, which, as is explained, only the eyes of faith can

see. Zen Buddhism goes to the point of saying that the experience of religious illumination, *satori*, is a "third eye," which opens to see things that the other two cannot see.

The sacred is established thanks to the power of the invisible. And it is invisible because religious language talks about the depths of the soul, the highest heaven and the hopelessness of hell, the fluids and influences that cure, Paradise, the eternal Beatitudes, and God himself. Who ever saw any of these entities?

You do not imagine a stone. It is visible, concrete. As such, it has nothing of the religious. But the moment someone gives it the name of "altar," it becomes surrounded with a mysterious aura, and the eyes of faith can envision invisible connections that connect it to the world of divine grace. And there you say your prayers and offer your sacrifices.

Bread, like other bread, wine, like other wine. They can be used in a common meal or in an orgy: they are entirely common material. They have no sacred odor arising from them. And the words are pronounced: "This is my body, this is my blood . . ."—and the visible objects acquire a new dimension and become signs of invisible realities.

I fear that my explanation might be convincing to religious people, but very weak to those who have never encountered the sacred. It is difficult to comprehend what this power means, this power of the invisible to which I am referring. I beg your permission, therefore, to use a parable, taken from the work of Antoine de Saint-Exupéry, *The Little Prince*. The prince had met an animal he had never seen before, a fox. At one point in their conversation, this is what happened between them. The fox is speaking.

"Please—tame me!" he said.

"I want to, very much," the little prince replied.
". . . What must I do, to tame you? . . ."

"You must be very patient," replied the fox.
"First you will sit down at a little distance from me—
like that—in the grass. . . . But you will sit a little closer
to me, every day. . . ."

So the little prince tamed the fox. And when the hour
of his departure drew near—

"Ah," said the fox, "I shall cry."

"It is your own fault," said the little prince. "I never
wished you any sort of harm; but you wanted me to
tame you . . . now you are going to cry! . . ."

"Then it has done you no good at all!"

"It has done me good," said the fox, "because of the
color of the wheat fields."

For the little fox had said to him once upon a time:

". . . You see the grain-fields down yonder? I do not eat
bread. Wheat is of no use to me. The wheat fields have
nothing to say to me. And that is sad. But you have hair
that is the color of gold. Think how wonderful that will
be when you have tamed me! The grain, which is also
golden, will bring me back the thought of you. And I
shall love to listen to the wind in the wheat. . . ." [Saint-
Exupéry: 67–68]

And the wheat, once without meaning, began to bear
within itself an absence that made the fox smile. It seems
to me that this parable presents, in paradigmatic form,
what religious discourse intends to do with things: transform them from simple and empty entities into carriers of
meaning, in such a manner that they become a part of the

human world, as if they were an extension of ourselves.

And we go on multiplying examples without end, relating the transformation of profane things into sacred things, to the extent that they become involved with the names of the invisible.

But it is necessary to pay attention to the differences. It so happens that religious discourse does not live within itself. It lacks the autonomy of natural things, which continue the same in whatever time, in whatever place. Religion is constructed with the symbols human beings use. But human beings are different. And their sacred worlds are different, too. "The world of the happy is different from the world of the unhappy" (Wittgenstein: 147). And so . . .

. . . There are those who make friends with nature, and recognize that they get life from it. And then they enfold, with the transparent veil of the invisible, the winds and the clouds, rivers and stars, animals and plants, sacramental places. And for this very reason they apologize to the animals that are going to be killed, to the branches that are going to be broken, to Mother Earth that will be excavated, and protect the springs from their excrement.

. . . There are also those who are companions of power and victory, who bless the sword, chains, armies, and their own laughter.

. . . There are sufferers, who transform the groans of the oppressed into psalms, swords into plowshares, spears into pruning-hooks, and construct, symbolically, utopias of peace and eternal justice, in which the wolf lives with the lamb and the child plays with the serpent.

What strange talk! It is good that we have to ask ourselves about this magic power that permits people to talk about what they have never seen. And the answer is that, for religion, it makes no difference what facts and actualities the five senses can grasp. What matters is the objects the *fantasy* and *imagination* can construct. Facts are not values, and actualities are not as valuable as love. Love is driven toward things as yet unborn, things absent. It lives on desire and hope. It is just here that *fantasy* and *imagination* arise, incantations calculated to produce the thing desired (Sartre: 159). We conclude, therefore, in all honesty, that *religious entities are imaginary entities*.

I know that such an assertion appears sacrilegious. Especially for people who have had an encounter with the sacred. For we learn quite early to identify the imagination with what is false. To affirm that someone's testimony is the product of the imagination and of fantasy is to accuse that person of mental problems, or to suspect his or her moral integrity. It might seem that the imagination is a mistake to be eradicated. In a special way for those who must survive in the institutional labyrinth, linguistic subtleties, and ritual pomp of the academic world, it is of basic importance that their speech be aseptically disinfected from any residue whatever of imagination and desire. Imagination must be subordinated to observation! Facts are to be taken as values. Object must triumph over desire! Everyone knows, in this scientific world, that imagination works against objectivity and the truth. How could anyone really committed to learning give in to the intoxication of desire and its end results?

No, I am not saying that religion is *only* imagination, *only* fantasy. On the contrary, I am suggesting that it has the power, the love, and the dignity of the imaginary. But, to elucidate a declaration so extravagant, we shall have to take a step backward, back to where culture is born and continues to be born. Why do we make flutes, invent dances, write poems, put flowers in our hair and necklaces around our necks, build houses, paint them happy colors, and put paintings on the walls? If we think that these human beings have been totally objective, totally dominated by facts, totally true—yes, totally true!—could they then have invented things? Where was the flute before it was invented? And the garden? And dances? And paintings? Absent. Nonexistent. No knowledge could possibly have pulled these things from nature. It was necessary that the imagination become pregnant in order that culture could be born. Therefore, in affirming that religious entities pertain to the imaginary, I am not ranging them with delusions and mental problems. I am only establishing their affiliation and recognizing the affinity that unites them.

We began by speaking of animals, of how they survive, of the adaptation of their bodies to the environment, and the adaptation of the environment to their bodies. Then we passed on to the human being, who does not survive by means of making physical adaptation, because he and she create culture, and with it the symbolical networks of religion.

And the reader will now have the right to ask us: But about these symbolical networks—We know that they are beautiful and have an aesthetic function. We know that from them are derived festivals and celebrations which establish their kinship with logical activities. But beyond this, what purpose do they serve? What good do they do for human beings? Aren't they only superfluous ornaments? Their survival depends on practical things and activities, material things like tools, weapons, food, work. Can symbols, entities so weak and transparent, born of imagination compete with the efficacy of that which is material and concrete?

Survival has to do with order. Observe the animals. They do nothing in isolation. There are no improvisations. For centuries and millennia their behavior has traced out

the same lines. When, for whatever reason, this order written in their organisms has collapsed, behavior loses its
unity and direction. And life ends.

Each animal has an order which is specific for it. Hum-
mingbirds do not survive in the same way that bulls do.
And it was while thinking of this that the biologist Jo-
hannes von Uexküll had the courage to wonder whether it
was really like that for animals—whether flies, butterflies,
sloths, and sea horses all live in the same world (Cassirer:
23–24). And we can imagine the environment as if it were a
great pipe organ, silent and at rest, and each organism a
musician that can make the instrument play its own specific melody. Thus there would be no environment-in-
itself. What there is for each animal is the world, created
in its own image and likeness, resulting from the activity of
each body upon what is around it. Each animal is a melody
which, if played, makes its surroundings reverberate with
the same harmonious notes and the same melodic theme.

The analogy does not work for everything, because we
know that we are not governed by our organisms. Our
music is not biological, but cultural. But in the same way
that the animal throws order over the world as if it were a
net (this order emanating from itself), searching for a
world in its image and likeness—in the same way it makes
its melody sound forth, and, resounding with it, the world
around it is awakened. The world's sounds are harmonious also. We throw out our nets, symbolical/religious—
our melodies—over the entire universe, to the outer
limits of time and the outer limits of space, in the
hope that the heavens and the earth will carry our values.
What is at stake is order. But not just any order will
meet human necessities. What is looked for, like hope
and utopia, as an unconscious project of the ego, is a

world that bears the marks of desire and that satisfies the aspirations of love. But the fact is that such a reality does not exist, not as something present. And religion appears as the grand hypothesis and wager that the entire universe has a human face. What science could construct such a horizon? The wings of imagination are necessary to articulate the symbols of absence. And we *say* religion, this symbolic universe. And "symbolic universes . . . proclaim that *all* reality is humanly meaningful and call upon the *entire* cosmos to signify the validity of human existence" (Berger and Luckmann: 96).

Human beings cannot plow the soil, beget children, or move machines with this. Symbols do not possess this type of efficacy. But they do meet another type of need, one as powerful as sex and hunger: the need to live in a world that makes sense. When the explanations that make sense collapse, we enter the world of insanity. Camus well said that the only philosophical problem is suicide, since it deals with the question of whether life is worth living or not. The problem is not material, but symbolical. It is not pain that disintegrates the personality, but the dissolution of explanations that make sense. This has been the tragic conclusion of the torture chambers. It is true that human beings do not live by bread alone. They also live by symbols, because without them there would be no order, no sense to life, and no will to live. If we could agree with the assertion that those who inhabit an ordered and meaningful world enjoy a sense of internal order, integration, unity, and direction, and feel a greater strength for living (Durkheim a: 464), we shall have discovered the effectiveness and the power of symbols, and envisioned the way in which imagination has contributed to the survival of humankind.

# CHAPTER THREE

# *The Exile of the Sacred*

*When we run over libraries, persuaded of these princi-*
*ples, what havoc we must make? If we take in our hand*
*any volume; of divinity or school metaphysics, for in-*
*stance; let us ask,* Does it contain any abstract reasoning
concerning quantity or number? *No.* Does it contain
any experimental reasoning concerning matter of fact
and existence? *No. Commit it then to the flames: for it*
*can contain nothing but sophistry and illusion. [Hume:*
*192–93]*

The things of the human world exhibit a curious property. We know that they are different from those that
constitute nature. The existence of water and air, the
alternation between day and night, the composition of
sulphuric acid, and the freezing-point of water in no way
depend upon the will of human beings. Even if we had
never existed, nature would be here, doing very well—
perhaps better. . . . With culture, things are different.
The transmission of inheritance, the sexual rights of men
and women, acts which constitute crimes and the punish-

ments imposed, decorations, money, property, language, the culinary art—all this has come from human beings' activity. When human beings disappear, these things will disappear also.

Here is the curious property to which we refer: We forget that cultural things were invented and for this reason appear to our eyes as if they were natural. In philosophical-sociological jargon this process has received the name of *reification*. It would be easier if we spoke of "*thingification*," because this is just what the word means, since it comes from the Latin *res*, which means "thing." Reification happens, in part, because children, when they are born, find a ready-made social world, as ready and as solid as nature. They do not see this world coming from their creative hands as if it were recently molded pottery from the potter's hands. Besides this, the older generation, concerned to preserve the fragile world which they have constructed with such care, is at pains to hide from younger ones, unconsciously, the artificial (and precarious) quality of the things that are here, because otherwise the young might begin to have dangerous ideas. In fact, if everything that constitutes the human world is artificial and conventional, then this world can be abolished and re-made in another form. But who would dare to think thoughts like this in relation to a world which had the solidity of natural things?

This applies in a special way to symbols. They are repeated and shared so much, they are so much used, successfully, under the guise of recipes, that we *reify* ("thingify") them—begin to treat them as if they were things. All symbols that are used successfully pass through this metamorphosis. They stop being hypotheses of the imagination and begin to be treated as manifestations of reality. Certain symbols derive their success from their power to convoke human beings, who use them to define their situation and articulate a common project of life. This is the case with ideologies, with utopias. Other symbols carry the day by their power to resolve practical problems, as in the case of magic and science. Victorious symbols, precisely because they are victorious, receive the name of "truth" while defeated symbols are ridiculed as superstitions or persecuted as heresies.

And we who want to know what religion is, who already know that it presents itself as a network of symbols—we have to stop for a moment to ask ourselves about what has happened to the symbols we have inherited. What have they done to us? What have we done to them? And to comprehend the process by which our symbols have become things and made a world, only to become old and fall apart later amid battles, we have to reconstruct a history. For it was in the midst of a history full of dramatic events, some grandiose, others quite small, that were forged the first and most passionate answers to the question, "What is religion?"

In the historical process, by means of which our civilization was formed, we received a religious-symbolic heritage, which came from two streams. On the one side were the Hebrews and Christians. On the other were the cultural traditions of the Greeks and Romans. With these symbols there came totally distinct visions of the world, but they came together, transforming each other, and came to flourish in the midst of the material conditions of life of the people who received them. And it was from this that there came the period of our history christened as the Middle Ages.

We know of no other epoch to which this period can be

compared. For here the symbols of the sacred acquired a density, a concreteness, and an omnipresence that made the invisible world closer and more felt than material realities. Nothing happened that was not by the power of the sacred, and everyone knew that the things of time were illuminated by the splendor and terror of eternity. It is not by accident that all medieval art should be dedicated to sacred things, and that nature never appears there as our eyes see it. Angels come to earth, the heavens appear connected to the world, while God presides over everything from the peak of his sublime height. And there were demonic possessions, witches and witchcraft, miracles, encounters with the devil, and good things happened because God protected those who feared him, and horrors and plagues were sent by him as punishment for sin and unbelief. All things had their proper place, in a hierarchy of values, because God had arranged the universe, his house, in that particular way, establishing spiritual guides and emperors on high to exercise power and use the sword, and placing poverty and work here below in other people's bodies.

Everything revolved around a central nucleus, a theme that unified everything: the drama of salvation, the fear of hell, the love of God taking pure souls to heaven. And it is perfectly comprehensible that such a drama demanded and established a geography that precisely located the dwelling-place of the demons and the blueprints of the mansions of the blessed.

If the universe had come from the hand of God by an act of personal creation (and it was even possible to determine with precision the date of this greatest of dates), and if God continued, by his grace, to sustain all things, one would conclude that everything, absolutely everything, had a *definite purpose*. And it was this teleological vision of reality (from *telos*, which, in Greek, means "end, purpose") which determined the fundamental question proposed by medieval science: "for what?" To know something was to know for what end it was destined. And the philosophers gave themselves over to the investigation of signs which in some way might indicate the meaning of each and of every thing. And so it was that a person named Kepler dedicated his life to the study of astronomy, in the firm conviction that God had not located the planets in the sky by accident. God was a great musical geometrician, and the mathematical regularities of the movements of the stars could be deciphered, so as to reveal the melody which God made the planets sing in chorus, in the firmament, for the ecstasy of human beings. At the end of his investigations, Kepler came to represent each of the planets by a musical note. What Kepler did in relation to the planets, others did with plants, rocks, animals, physical and chemical phenomena, asking themselves about their aesthetic, ethical, human finalities. In fact, their finality was just this: the entire universe was comprehended as something endowed with human meaning. And precisely here one finds its essential religious character.

Here I shall entertain a parenthesis. I can imagine the reader smiling, shocked at this kind of imagination. Strange, but it is always this way: from within their enchanted world, fantasies always present themselves with the solidity of mountains. For the medieval person this was no fantasy at all. Their world was solid, constituted by facts, proved by abundant evidence, and beyond any doubt. The medievals' attitude toward their world was identical to our attitude toward our world. Like them, we are incapable of recognizing what is fantasy in what we

judge to be solid terrain, *terra firma*. And the fascinating
thing is that a civilization built of fantasies should have
survived for so many centuries. And in that civilization
men and women lived, worked, fought, built cities, made
music, painted pictures, erected cathedrals. It is stange
that this power of fantasy could construct webs strong
enough for people to dwell upon.

Few there were who doubted. Recipes that produce
cakes that taste good are not questioned. When a given
system of symbols functions in an adequate manner,
doubts do not appear. The recipe is rejected when the cake
regularly comes out hard; doubt and questioning come in
when an action is frustrated in its objectives. Those who
doubt, or propose new systems of ideas, are mad, or ignorant, or irreverent iconoclasts.

It happened, however, that little by little, but constantly, progressively, in a growing way, men and women
began to do things which had not been provided for in the
religious cookbook. It was not those at the top of the sacred hierarchy who did them. And neither were they those
who were condemned to the cellars. Those who are on top
rarely undertake different things. They are not interested
in changing things. Power and riches are benevolent toward those who possess them. Those who find themselves
quite underneath, crushed by the weight of the situation,
spend their few energies in the simple struggle for a little
bread. To avoid death by starvation is something of
triumph. It was from a social class that formed itself in the
middle that there came a new and subversive economic
attitude that ate through the things and the symbols of the
medieval world.

By contrast with the citizens of the sacred world, who
had created symbols that permitted them to *comprehend*

reality as a drama and to visualize their place within the plot, for the new class the interest was in *activities*, like production, commerce, making work rational, travelling to discover new markets, to get profits, to create wealth. And, if the former found their identity in terms of the divine marks they possessed by birth, the latter affirmed: "By birth we are nothing. We have made ourselves. We are what we produce." And thus was contrasted the sacred uselessness of those who occupied the privileged places of medieval society, with the practical usefulness of those who, without marks of birth, were nevertheless capable of altering the face of the world by means of their work. In the name of the principle of usefulness, tradition, in a systematic manner, will be sacrificed to the rationality of the production of wealth. That which is not useful ought to perish.

To the same extent that utilitarianism was imposed and began to govern peoples' activities, an enormous revolution was occurring in the field of symbols. Some think that this occurred because of people's understanding that symbols are copies, reflections, echoes of what we do. If this were true, symbols would not be any more than effects of material causes, and would be empty of any type of efficacy at all. It so happens that, as we have already suggested, symbols are not mere ideal entities. They gain density, invade the world, and here place themselves alongside hoes and weapons. Because of this, I reject the notion that they are a mere translation, in other terminology, of the material forms of society and its vital necessities. What happens is that, as new problems arise, relative to concrete life, people are almost obliged to *invent* new conceptual formulas. There has then been produced a *new orientation for thought*, derived from a new *will to manipulate and control* nature. The medieval person wanted to contemplate and understand. His or her attitude was passive, receptive. Now the necessity of wealth inaugurated an aggressive, active attitude, by which the new class appropriated nature—manipulating it, controlling it, forcing nature to submit to their intentions, fitting it into the pipeline that goes from the mines and the fields to the factories and from there to the markets. And silently the triumphant bourgeoisie wrote the epitaph for the dying sacral order: "Until now religious people have sought to understand nature; but what counts is not to understand it, but to transform it."

What has happened to the religious universe?

The religious universe had been enchanted. An enchanted world harbors within its breast powers and possibilities which escape our capacities to explain, to manipulate, to forecast. One is dealing, therefore, with something which can never be completely understood by the power of reason, and never completely rationalized and organized by the power of work.

But how can the project of the bourgeoisie survive in a world like this, a world obscured by mysteries, a world in which anarchy is created by the unexpected? The intention was to produce, in a rational way, increased wealth. This demanded the establishment of an instrument of investigation that would produce the needed results. And what instrument freer of irrational religious presupposition— what more universal, more transparent instrument—could exist than mathematics? Here was a language totally empty of mysteries, totally dominated by reason—an ideal instrument for the construction of a world likewise empty of mysteries and dominated by reason. As for the religious world, since practical human activity can only be exercised upon visible objects and material properties, the invisible entities of the religious world cannot have any function to fulfill in this universe. And I would invite you to return to the short citation from Hume that I have placed at the head of this chapter, as it clearly reveals the spirit of this utilitarian world that established itself and the destiny it reserved for the symbols of the imagination: the flames.

Nature has lost its sacred aura. The heavens do not declare the glory of God, as Kepler believed, neither does the earth sound forth his love. Heaven and earth are not the poem of an invisible Supreme Being. And it is because of this that there is no interdict, no prohibition, no taboo against laying siege to them. Nature is nothing more than a source of raw goods, a brute entity, destitute of value. Respect for rivers and springs, that could prevent their being polluted, respect for the forest, that could keep it from being cut down, respect for the air and for the sea, that could demand that they be preserved, have no place in the symbolic universe established by the bourgeoisie. Its utilitarianism knows only *profit* as the standard for evaluating things. And even people lose their religious value. In the medieval world, however devalued they were, their value was something absolute, because it was conferred upon them by God himself. Now persons are worth what they earn, while they earn.

Much of what people think about religion has its origins in this conflict. And the answers given to the question, "What is religion?" have much to do with the loyalties of the people involved. The condemnation of the sacred was demanded by the interests of the bourgeoisie and the advance of secularization. This conflict is not actually circumscribed in a precise way; it is not contained within strict limits of time and space, because it returns and stays alive at the frontiers of expansion of capitalism and wherever the dynamic of the production of profits collides with the sacral worlds. Just pick up the newspaper and be advised of the tensions between Church and State, Church and economic interests. The arguments are the same. The ideas are repeated. Let religion take care of spiritual realities, and the sword and money will take care of things!

It is necessary to recognize that religion represented the past: tradition. It dealt with a form of knowledge which had come from the midst of a defeated social and political organization.

Science, for its part, aligned itself with the sinners and was supported by them. Its methods and conclusions turned out to be extraordinarily well-adapted to the logic of the bourgeois world. What mattered to science, more than anything else (not to say exclusively), was to know how things functioned. Knowledge is *to know how things function*. And the one who knows how things function has the secret of manipulation and control. And this is how this kind of knowledge opens the way for technology, making the connection between the university and the factory, the factory and profit. And what a long way we are from medieval science, which asked itself about the ultimate *purpose* of things and sought to hear harmonies and behold divine purpose in the happenings of the world!

The success of science was total. Successful things cannot be questioned. How can efficiency be doubted? The conclusion is ineluctable: science is on the side of the truth. Knowledge can only come to us through the avenue of the scientific method. And this means, more than anything else, rigorous objectivity. Submission of the thought to the fact, subordination of the imagination to observation. Facts are elevated to the category of values.There is established a kind of discourse whose only purpose is to say the observable. The things that are said and thought must correspond to the things that are seen and perceived. This is truth.

And religious discourse? A statement of absences, denial of the facts, creation of the imagination: this can be classified only as conscious deceit or mental aberration. Because if it does not "contain any abstract reasoning concerning quantity or number . . ." or "contain any experimental reasoning concerning matter of fact and existence, . . . it can contain nothing but sophistry and illusion."

Worse than a statement of falsehood is discourse destitute of sense. If I say, "Fire is cold," I am uttering a falsehood. I am saying something that anyone can understand—only it is not true. But, if I say "Fire, in all probability, darkened the silence," the reader will be nonplussed, and say, "I know all the words, one by one. But the thing doesn't make sense." For an enunciated statement to be declared false it is necessary that it make sense. But science did not even concede falsehood to religion. It declared that religion's discourse did not make sense, because it referred to imaginary entities.

Thus was established a symbolic framework in which there was no place for religion. Religion was identified with the past, with backwardness, with the ignorance of a black period of history, the Dark Ages, and explained as the infantile behavior of unevolved people and groups, as illusion, opium, neurosis, ideology. By contrast with this sinister picture: a future bright with progress, wealth, and scientific knowledge. And so there were not a few who wrote up premature obituaries of the sacred, and made prophecies of religion's disappearance and the advent of a social order totally secularized and profane.

But if this picture of the interpretation of religious phenomenon was established, it was because in fact religion had lost its power and centrality. As Rickert said, with the triumph of the bourgeoisie God started having chronic housing problems. Evicted from one place, evicted from another. Progressively God was pushed out of the world. For human beings to dominate the earth it was necessary that God be confined to heaven.

And so the areas of influence were divided.

To the businessmen and politicians were given the land, the seas, the rivers, the air, the fields, the cities, the factories, the banks, the markets, the profits, and peoples' bodies.

Religion was assigned the administration of the invisible world, the care of salvation, the cure of tormented souls.

It is strange that there was still space for religion. It is strange that the facts of economy did not liquidate the sacred once for all. It appears, however, that there are certain anthropological realities that endure despite everything. People continue to have nights of insomnia and to think about life and about death. And businessmen and bankers also have souls. It is not enough for them to have possession of wealth; they want to raise over it the banners of religion. They want assurance that their wealth has been deserved, and they seek in wealth the signs of divine favor and encircle it with confessions of piety.

It is not by accident that the most powerful coins represent themselves as the most pious, having engraved upon themselves the statement: "In God We Trust."

And the factory workers and farm laborers, too, have souls, and need to hear the songs of heaven in order to bear the sadness of earth. And the sacred has survived also as the religion of the oppressed.

# CHAPTER FOUR

# *The Thing That Never Lies*

*There are no religions which are false. . . . All answer,
though in different ways, to the given conditions of
human existence. [Durkheim a:15]*

In the world of people we find two types of things.

In the first place, there are *things that signify or suggest
other things:* these are "symbol-things." A wedding ring
signifies marriage; a banknote signifies a value; a statement signifies a state of things, something other than itself. But someone can wear a wedding ring on the left hand
without being married. A banknote can be a counterfeit. A
statement can be a lie. Because of this, when we are confronted with things that signify other things, it is inevitable
that we raise questions about their truth or falsity.

Next, there are *things that do not signify or suggest
other things.* They are themselves—they do not point to
anything else, they are devoid of additional meaning. I
drink a glass of water. The water kills thirst. That's
enough for me. Don't ask me if the water is truthful. It is
crystal clear, cold, delicious. . . . Fire is fire. What does it
signify? Nothing. It signifies itself. It warms, illuminates,
burns. To ask if it is truthful makes no sense. That flower,

there in the middle of the garden, born by accident when the wind carried a seed, also signifies nothing else. A flower is a flower. Concerning a flower—as with all things that do not signify other things—I cannot raise a question about truth, an epistemological question. But I can ask if it has a pleasant scent, if it is beautiful, if it is perfect.

Things that signify nothing else can be transformed into symbols. The fox can become happy looking at a wheat field. Fire, too, is transformed into a symbol on altar candles or olympic pyres. And the flower can be a declaration of love or a statement of loneliness, if cast upon a tomb.

Things that symbolize nothing can come to signify something by means of a device: all we have to do is write something on them, as sweethearts carve their names on tree trunks, and as do those who, believing in their own importance, have commemorative plaques with their names in large letters put upon the pyramids and viaducts they have had constructed.

Sometimes even words, "symbol-things" par excellence, are transformed into things. Art helps us to understand this. Looking at a painting or a sculpture, it is easy to see that there are symbols that signify scenery or a person. Thus, the degree of *"truth"* of a work of art would be measured by its fidelity in copying the original. What does a work of architecture copy? It copies nothing. It is a matter of a construction which the artist makes, using certain materials, and this work becomes a thing among other things. A canvas of Picasso must have a low degree of truth. It is nothing like the original. Could we not raise the hypothesis that the artist in plastics is not in search of the truth with respect to the conformity of his work to the original, but, on the contrary, that he is *constructing a thing*, itself and unique?

Someone asked Beethoven, after he had played one of

his compositions on the piano: "What do you want to say in this musical piece? What does it mean?"

He replied, "What does it mean? What do I want to say? That's simple." Beethoven sat down at the piano and played the same piece.

It didn't mean anything. It was not a symbol-thing that signified something else. It was the thing, itself.

Architects, artists in plastics, musicians, construct things using bricks, paint and bronze, sounds. And there are those who construct things using words. Meditate upon this statement of Archibald Macleish.

> A Poem should be palpable and mute
> As a globed fruit . . .
> A poem should be wordless
> As the flight of birds. . . .
> A poem should not mean
> But be. [Archibald Macleish: 471]

I remember how, as a boy in a city of Brazil's interior, I used to hear the men swapping stories after dinner. The stories were tall tales, and they all knew this. But I never heard one of them say to the other: "You are lying." The appropriate reaction to a tall tale was different: "Why that's nothing." And the new artist began the construction of another *object of words*. It didn't take me long to realize that, in that game, the criteria of *truth and falsity* didn't apply. For the things that were said did not *signify* anything else. The things were said in order to *construct* objects, which could be beautiful, fascinating, funny, grotesque, fantastic—but never false.

There are certain situations in which words no longer denote anything: they abandon the realm of truth and falsity and start to exist alongside things.

The person who confuses *things that signify something else* with things that signify nothing is committing a serious mistake.

The works of Bach were discovered accidentally when they were being used to wrap meat in a butcher-shop. The butcher did not understand the symbols; he could not understand the written text and, consequently, he could not hear the music. For him the only reality was the thing—the paper—quite useful for wrapping.

Medieval science looked at the universe and thought that it was an ensemble of things that signified other things. Each planet was a symbol. For us to hear the message they carried the symbols had to be deciphered. And Kepler tried to discover the musical harmonies of these worlds. Physics only went forward when the universe was recognized as a thing. And it was thus that Galileo stopped asking what the universe signified and concentrated simply upon asking what it was and how it functioned and what were the laws which governed it.

Whoever would undertake to understand the function of the dollar from the writing printed on bills would arrive at comical conclusions. The dollar is not to be understood from the *meaning* of "In God We Trust," but from its *performance as a thing* in the economic world.

This was what the empirical positivists did with religion. They ignored it as a *social thing* and concentrated upon the statements and affirmations that appear together with it. They concluded that religious discourse was without real meaning—a conclusion as trite as affirming that water, fire, and flowers have no meaning. It never entered their minds that words could be used for anything except to denote. They did not perceive that words can be the raw materials with which worlds are built.

The situation is ironic. In the Middle Ages the philosophers, from within their religious perspective, wanted to see messages written in the sky. They contemplated the universe as a text endowed with meaning. But science did not emerge from its impasse until it recognized that stars and planets are *things*: they signify nothing else.

Now the situation is inverted. The empirical positivists are the ones who are insisting on interpreting religion as a text, ignoring it as a thing.

And it is then that the sociological revolution occurred. A radical change of perspective. And a new world of the understanding of religion was established with the statement: *"Consider social facts as things"* (Durkheim b: 14).

Durkheim also wrote:

It is said that science denies religion in principle. But religion exists; it is a system of given facts; in a word, it is a reality. How could science deny this reality? [Durkheim a: 478]

Now if religion is a fact, the judgment of truth and falsity cannot be applied to it.

"There are no religions which are false" (ibid., p. 15), he says, horrifying empiricists and priests, blasphemers and fanatics. Religion is an institution, and no institution can be built upon error or upon a lie. "If it were not founded in the nature of things, it would have encountered in the facts a resistance over which it could never have triumphed" (ibid., p. 14).

And in the "Conclusion" of his work on religious life:

Our entire study rests upon this postulate that the unanimous sentiment of the believers of all times cannot be purely illusory. Together with a recent apologist of the faith ["William James, *The Varieties of Religious Experience*"] we admit that these religious beliefs rest upon a specific experience whose demonstrative value is, in one sense, not one bit inferior to that of scientific experiments, though different from them. [ibid., pp. 464–65]

All would agree that it would be unscientific to denounce the law of gravity upon the allegation that so many people have died in falls. If we proceed in this fashion in relation to the facts of the physical universe, why do we act differently in relation to the facts of the human universe? First of all one must understand. And we already have a suspicion: contradicting those who imagined that religion was a passing phenomenon, on its way to extinction, its universality and persistence suggest to us that it reveals "an essential and permanent aspect of humanity."

What are religions? At first sight we are shocked by the immense varieties of rites and myths that we find in them, which makes us think that perhaps it would be impossible to discover a feature common to them all. Yet, just as in a game of chess the variety of moves are all made upon a square chessboard divided into black and white spaces, so religions, without any exception, establish a two-part division of the entire universe that splits it into two classes containing everything that exists. And in that way we find the space of *sacred things* and, separated from them by a series of prohibitions, *secular or profane things*.

Sacred and profane are not properties of things. They are established by our attitude toward things, spaces, times, people, actions.

The profane world is the circle of utilitarian attitudes. What is a utilitarian attitude? When my ballpoint gets old, I throw it away. I do the same with rusty nails. A medication whose expiration date has come is thrown into the garbage. We used to use a cloth filter to make coffee. Afterwards, paper filters appeared—more "practical"—and the old ones were retired as no longer useful. Then inflation made the old cloth filters more practical than those of paper. The cloth ones are more economical. In a utilitarian world there is nothing permanent. Everything has become disposable. The criterion of utility takes away from things and from people all the value they might have in themselves, and takes into consideration only whether or not they can be used. That is how the economy works. In fact, the circle of the profane and the circle of the economical coincide. What is not useful is abandoned. But what about the individual who judges whether or not a certain thing is useful? This is an area in which individuals are still their own rulers. No one can tell them what to do. To the extent that the profane and secular world advances, individualism and utilitarianism advance also.

In the sacred sphere everything is transformed. In the secular realm the individual was the governor of things, the center of the world. Now, to the contrary, things possess the person. One is not the center of anything and finds oneself *totally dependent* upon something superior to oneself (Schleiermacher: 13–14). One feels oneself tied to sacred things by cords of profound reverence and respect. The person is inferior, the sacred is superior: it is an object of adoration. The sacred is the creator, the origin of life, the source of power. We are creatures, in search of life, lacking in power. The utilitarian criteria are abandoned. We are no longer the center of the world, not the decision-makers, not even our own rulers. We feel ourselves dominated and enveloped by something more powerful than we, something that imposes upon us norms of behavior that cannot be transgressed, *even if they do not demonstate any utility*. In fact, going against the criterion of utility is one of the marks of the realm of the sacred. Fasting, forgiving, the refusal to kill sacred animals to eat, self-flagellation, and, in its most extreme form, self-sacrifice—all of these are practices which are not defined by their utility, but simply by the sacred density which religion attributes to them. And this is what makes them obligatory.

Durkheim did not investigate religion gratuitously, for mere curiosity. He lived in a world that showed signs of disintegration, a world that was split by all of the problems stemming from the expansion of capitalism—problems similar to ours. And this was what led him to the question: How can there be a society? What mysterious power is this that keeps isolated individuals—each of them pursuing his or her own interests, which conflict with those of others—from destroying each other? Why don't they devour each other? What is the source of the relative harmony of social life?

The answer that had been previously proposed to this question said that individuals, motivated by their interests, had created society as a *means* for their satisfaction. The individual makes the decision—society comes later. The individual is at the center—society is the system revolving around him or her. All of this fits well into that utilitarian, pragmatic scheme of the secular world, as indicated. And, still further, if society is a *means*, it is almost in the very condition of things that can be discarded when they lose their utility.

The problem is that social life, as we know it, does not fit into this secular and utilitarian framework. The most serious things that we do have nothing to do with utility.

They result from our reverence and respect for norms that we did not create, that constrain us, that drive us to our knees. . . . From the strictly utilitarian point of view it would be more economical to kill old people, castrate the bearers of genetic defects, kill handicapped children, abort accidental and undesired pregnancies, make political adversaries disappear, shoot criminals and possible criminals. But something tells us that these things *ought not to be done*. Why? Because, that's why. For moral reasons, without utilitarian justifications. And even when we do such things, without being caught, there is a voice, a feeling of guilt, a conscience, that tells us that something sacred has been violated.

What occurs when secularization advances, utilitarianism imposes itself, and the sacred dissolves? Robbed of that sacred center that demands the reverence of individuals for norms of social life, people lose their points of reference. *Anomie* prevails. And society shatters under the growing pressure of the centrifugal force of individualism. If it is possible to break the norms, take one's advantage and escape unharmed, what utilitarian argument can be invoked to avoid crime?

The sacred is the center of the world, the origin of order, the source of norms, the guarantee of harmony. Thus, when Durkheim explored religion, he was investigating the very conditions for the survival of social life. And this is what his most revolutionary conclusion affirms about the essence of religion.

What is the thing mysteriously present at the center of the sacred sphere? Where do the religious experiences come from—the experiences which we explain and describe with widely varied names and differing myths? What do we find at the center of religious imagery?

The answer is not difficult. We are born weak and defenseless, unable to survive as isolated individuals. We receive from society a name and an identity. From society we learn to think and to become rational. By society we are welcomed, protected, fed. And finally, it is society that will mourn our death. It is understandable that this may be the God whom all religions adore, even if in a hidden form, concealed from the eyes of the faithful. Thus, "this reality, which mythologies have represented under so many different forms, but which is the universal and eternal objective cause of these sensations *sui generis* out of which religious experience is made, *is society*" (Durkheim a: 465, emphasis added).

To the faithful it matters little whether their ideas are correct or not. The essence of religion is not the idea, but the power. "The believer who has communicated with his god is not merely a man who sees new truths of which the unbeliever is ignorant; he is a man who is *stronger*. He feels within him more force, either to endure the trials of existence, or to conquer them" (ibid., p. 464). The sacred is not a sphere of knowledge, but a sphere of power.

Durkheim perceives that consciousness of the sacred only appears by virtue of the human capacity to imagine, to think of, an ideal world. We do not see this in animals, which exist submerged exclusively in facts. Human beings, on the contrary, contemplate facts and clothe them with a sacred aura which never appears as a crude fact, appearing only by its capacity to conceive the ideal and to add something to reality. Indeed, *the ideal and the sacred are the same thing*.

Durkheim's certainty that religion was the center of society was so great that he could not imagine a society that would be completely profane and secularized.

Wherever there is a society, there will be gods and sacred experiences. And he even went to the point of asserting:

> There is something eternal in religion which is destined to survive all the particular symbols in which religious thought has successively enveloped itself. There can be no society which does not feel the need of upholding and reaffirming at regular intervals the collective sentiments and the collective ideas which make its unity and its personality. [ibid., pp. 474–75]

Religion may be transformed. But it will never disappear. And Durkheim concludes by recognizing a void and proclaiming a hope: "The old gods are growing old or already dead, and others are not yet born" (ibid., p. 475). Nevertheless, "a day will come when our societies will know again those hours of creative effervescence, in the course of which new ideas arise and new formulae are found which serve for a while as a guide to humanity" (ibid.).

# CHAPTER FIVE

## *Flowers on Chains*

Religious *distress is at the same time the* expression *of real distress and the* protest *against real distress. Religion is the sigh of the oppressed creature, the heart of a heartless world, just as it is the spirit of a spiritless situation. It is the* opium *of the people. [Marx and Engels b: 42]*

We enter into another world. Durkheim contemplated the faint colors of the disappearing world, as dusky clouds at sunset, changing from rose to black in the rapid changes of the sinking sun. Fascinated, he undertook the search for its origins, the search for a long ago time. And there he sought the simplest and most primitive religion known, in the hope that the sacred-totemic world of the Australian aborigines would offer us visions of a paradise—a social order built around spiritual and moral values. The past penetrated in order to understand the present. To understand with hope.

Marx does not live in the twilight. He is already in the darkness of night. He walks among the ruins. He analyzes the dissolution. He develops the study of capital and

46

diagnoses its end. He has nothing to preach and offers no advice. He seeks no lost paradises because he does not believe in them. But he directs his gaze toward future horizons and hopes for the coming of the Holy City, a society without oppressed and oppressors—a society of liberty, of the erotic transfiguration of the body.

But the ground on which he walks knows nothing of the sacral world, nothing of moral norms and spiritual values. Secularized from beginning to end, it knows only the profit ethic and the enthusiasm of capital and wealth. It makes no difference that the capitalists go to church buildings and say prayers, or that they build holy cities or support missionary efforts, or yet that there is holy water at the official opening of factories and thanksgiving services for their prosperity, or, much less, that masses are said for the eternal salvation of their souls. This world knows nothing of spiritual elements. Salaries and prices are established neither by religion nor by ethics. Wealth is built by means of a strictly material logic: the logic of profit, which knows no compassion. Indeed those who have compassion condemn themselves to destruction. You cannot deny that the gestures and the speeches still refer to gods and to moral values: make-up, incense, deodorants, perfumes, a sacred aura that wraps everything in its fragrance without altering anything. And Marx has to insist on a rigorously materialistic conduct of the analysis. In fact, materialism is demanded by the system which knows only the power of material factors. It is the logic of profit and wealth that makes it this way—and not the personal inclinations of those who make the analysis.

Few know that Marx's view of religion took form and was developed in the midst of a political battle that was being waged. And the battle was not with clerics or with

theologians, but with a group of philosophers who understood that religion was the biggest culprit of all the social
miseries of that day. This group wanted to establish an
educational program with the objective of getting people
to abandon their religious illusions. Marx was convinced
that religion bore no guilt at all. And he was convinced
that nothing was more impossible than the elimination of
ideas, even false ones, from peoples' heads. And I imagine
that clerics and religious people may rub hands in glee:
"Finally we have discovered a Marx on our side."

Nothing could be further from the truth. Religion was
not guilty for the simple reason that it made no difference
at all. How could a eunuch be accused of deflowering a
virgin? How could religion be accused of responsibility if
it were nothing more than a shadow, an echo, an inverted
image projected upon a wall? It was not the *cause* of anything. A *symptom*, perhaps. And because of this, the philosophers who had presented themselves as dangerous
revolutionaries were nothing more than replicas of Don
Quixote, tilting at windmills.

Marx did not want to waste energy on paper dragons.
He was in search of the powers which really drive society.
For it was there, and only there, that the battles should be
fought.

What were these powers?

The revolutionary philosophers to whom we refer, left-
wing Hegelians, wanted society to undergo radical trans-
formations. And they understood that the social order was
built with a mortar in which material things were cemented
to each other by means of ideas and thought-forms. Thus,
weapons, machines, banks, factories, lands, were all held
together by religion, law, philosophy, theology. The
political-tactical conclusion necessarily followed: if there

were an attitude able to dissolve ideas and modify old thought forms, the entire social edifice would begin to tremble. And thus it was that the "young Hegelians" decided to fight the revolutionary battles on the fields of ideas, using as a weapon something that in that time was called *criticism*. Today, possibly, they would speak of "conscientization." And they mounted an assault against religion.

Marx laughed at this. The Hegelians see things upside down. They think that ideas are the causes of social life, when they are nothing more than effects that appear after things happen. It was not consciousness that determined life, Marx held. It was life that determined consciousness. And he asserted: "The phantoms formed in the brains of men are also, necessarily, sublimates of their material life-process, which is empirically verifiable and bound to material premises" (Marx and Engels a: 42). For:

The production of ideas, of conceptions, of consciousness, is at first directly interwoven with the material activity and the material intercourse of men—the language of real life. Conceiving, thinking, the mental intercourse of men at this stage still appear as the direct efflux of their material behaviour. The same applies to mental production as expressed in the language of the politics, laws, morality, religion, metaphysics, etc., of a people. [ibid.]

"*Man makes religion*," said Marx, "religion does not make man" (Marx and Engels b: 41). It is fire that makes smoke; smoke does not make fire.

And just as it is useless to try to put out a fire by blowing the smoke away, it is also useless to try to change the con-

ditions of life by a criticism of religion. Our consciousness
of smoke directs us to the fire from which it comes. In
exactly the same way, our consciousness of religion forces
us to consider the material conditions that produce it.

Who is this human being who makes religion?

He and she are a body, a body that has to eat, a body
that needs clothes and living-quarters, a body that repro-
duces, a body that has to transform nature, to work, to
survive.

But a body does not float on thin air. We do not find a
body in an abstract or universal form. We see people indis-
solubly tied to the world, where one has to fight for survival, and bearing in their bodies the marks of nature and
the marks of tools. The laborers, the fishermen, the farm
workers, the construction-workers, the bus-drivers, those
who work at forges and presses, those who teach children
and adults to read—all of these, each in a specific way,
bear in their bodies the marks of their work. Marks that
translate into the food they can afford to eat, the illnesses
they can have, the entertainment they can afford, the years
they can live, and the thoughts they can dream about—
their religions and their hopes.

Marx also dreamed and imagined. And although some
consider him more important because of the economic
science that he founded, belittling his flights of fantasy as
juvenile ecstasies, I place myself among those who turn
things around and dwell especially on those frontiers at
which his thought invades the horizons of utopias. And
Marx asked himself about another kind of work that
would give pleasure and happiness to people—work similar to the creations of artists and the non-utilitarian
pleasure of playing and sport, work as an expression of
freedom, activity which is spiritually creative, builder of a

world in harmony with its intention. It is clear that Marx had never seen this utopian dream realized in any society. It was his construction, beginning from small fragments of experience, shaped by memory and by hope. But these are the utopian horizons, which sharpen our vision so that we can perceive the absurdities of the *topos*, the place where we live. And when he contemplated work, what he discovered was *alienation*, from beginning to end.

What is alienation?

To alienate property means to transfer to another person the possession of something that belongs to us. I have a house: I can give it away or sell it to someone else. By this process it is alienated. An alienation, therefore, is not something that happens in peoples' heads. It has to do with an objective, external process of the transfer from one person to another of something that has belonged to the first party.

Why is work marked by alienation?

Let us return for an instant to work which is not alienated—work that is creative, free, as Marx imagined. Its essential mark is this. The person desires something. This desire stimulates the imagination, which visualizes what is desired, whether a garden, a symphony, or a simple toy. Imagination and desire inform the body, which gives itself wholly to work, out of love for the object to be created. And when the work is over, the creator contemplates his or her work, sees that it is very good, and rests.

What happens to those who work within our present conditions?

In the first place, they have to alienate their desire. Another's desire has now become their desire. They work for someone else.

In the second place, the object to be produced is not the

result of their decision. They are not fathering a child for themselves. Indeed they are not involved in the production of any object, because with the division of production into a series of specialized and independent acts, they are lowered from the condition of builders of things to the condition of someone who simply tightens a screw, pushes a button, or wields a hammer. If you ask workers at an automobile factory, "What do you do?" no one will say, "I make automobiles. Have you seen the nice cars I make?" They won't tell you what objects they make, but what specialized function their bodies perform, "I'm a machinist. I'm a toolmaker. I'm an electrician."

In the third place, and as a consequence of what has already been said, work is not an activity that brings pleasure, but an activity that brings suffering. People work because they have no other alternative. Forced work. The greatest ideal, retirement. They will find their pleasure outside work. And for this they will submit to work and to their salary.

Finally, work creates a world independent of the will of workers . . . and capitalists. For the capitalists are also alienated. They cannot do what they wish. All of their conduct is rigorously determined by the law of profit. It is not difficult to understand how this happens. Let us imagine that you, knowing that the good part of capitalism is to be a capitalist, and having a certain amount in savings, resolve to try your wings and invest in the stock market. How will you go about it? You should consult the stock market averages to learn of the best investment. And what will you find in these averages? Numbers, nothing more. Numbers show the possibilities for profits. If the firms in which you are going to invest are levelling forests and causing ecological devastation, if they are prospering by the production of weapons, if they are unjust and cruel with their employees, all this is absolutely irrelevant. Once the profit motive is established, everything from thalidomide to napalm is transformed into merchandise, including the worker. This is the secular world, governed by the money motive. And what occurs is that the world established by the logic of profits—which includes everything from ecological devastation to war—is totally alienated, separated from the desires of people, who perhaps would have preferred something simpler. Thus green acres are delivered to real estate speculation; the Indians lose their lands because cattle is better for the economy than Indians; the lands become muddy swamps, while the rivers and seas become poisonous soup, and the fish float, dead.

But what factors lead workers to accept such a situation? Why do they work in this alienated way? Why don't they move out into something else?

Because there is no alternative. They possess only their bodies. In order to produce they must couple themselves to machines, the means of production. The machines and the means of production are not theirs and are governed by the profit motive. And so it is that the very concept of alienation reveals to us a society divided into two groups. Two social classes. Two completely different ways for the body to be. Workers are coupled to machines, and because of this have to follow the machines' rhythm and do what they demand. This will leave marks on the hands, the posture, the face, the eyes . . . especially the eyes. The bodies that live in the world of profit also have their marks, that range from their white collars and ties, to the restaurants they frequent, to the romantic affairs they maintain, to the cardiovascular infirmities that afflict them.

And it is not necessary to think very long to understand

that the interests of these two classes are not harmonious. For Marx, here is to be found the greatest contradiction of capitalism: capitalism grows thanks to a condition that makes a conflict between workers and employers inevitable. Marx never *advocated* class war. He thought such a situation detestable. He was only like a physician who diagnoses a sick patient. He said: The end result is inevitable because the organs are at war. The problem is not of a moral or psychological nature. It will not be resolved by good will on the part of the workers and generosity on the part of the employers. No salary, however high it might be, will eliminate the alienation. We are dealing according to the viewpoint of Marx with a law, as inflexible as the law of chemistry that says: compress the volume of a gas, and the pressure increases, expand the volume and the pressure falls. And here we could state: "compressing salaries to their minimum produces economic miracles expanded to the maximum."

This is a reality: men and women working, together with others, under conditions that they do not want. . . . And it is from this come echoes, dreams, screams and groans, poems, philosophies, utopias, aesthetic criteria, laws, constitutions, religions.

> Above fire, smoke
> Above reality, voices
> Above infrastructure, superstructure
> Above life, consciousness.

Only, everything appears upside down, confused. Marx said, there in *Das Kapital*, that we only see clearly when we make things from beginning to end, in accordance with a previously sketched plan. But who makes things from beginning to end? Who understands the overall plan? Presidents? Planners? The President's Cabinet? The World Monetary Fund?

It is understood that what people normally have in their heads is not knowledge, or science, but pure *ideology*, smoke, secretions, reflections of an absurd world.

And it is here that religion appears, partly to enlighten the dark corners of knowledge. But, pity religion, the poor thing. Religion itself cannot see. How can it pretend to enlighten anything? It enlightens with *illusions* that console the weak and *legitimations* that strengthen the powerful.

Religion is the general theory of that world,
its encyclopaedic compendium,
its logic in a popular form,
its spiritualistic *point d'honneur,*
its enthusiasm,
its moral sanction,
its solemn completion,
its universal ground for consolation and justification.
[Marx and Engels b: 41]

Indeed, when the oppressed poor, from the depths of suffering, stammer, "It's God's will," all logical reasons and arguments are over, injustices are transformed into mysteries of unsearchable designs, and their own misery into a trial which is to be supported with patience, in the hope of eternal salvation for their souls. And the powerful use the same sacred words and invoke the divine power as an accomplice in war and plundering. And the original inhabitants of this continent and their civilizations were massacred in the name of the cross, and colonial expan-

sion took with it to Africa and Asia the God of the whites
and the constitutions they wrote invoking the will of God,
and a representative of God goes alongside the one condemned to die. . . . Nothing is changed, nothing is transformed, but over all the things of humankind is spread the
aroma of incense. . . .
  Religion,

> the *expression* of real distress
> and the *protest* against real distress.
> . . . the sigh of the oppressed creature,
> the heart of a heartless world,
> . . . the spirit of a spiritless situation
> . . . the *opium* of the people. [Marx and Engels b: 42]

And in this way the words growing out of suffering are
themselves transformed into a temporary balm for a pain
which religion is unable to cure. That is why it is opium,
"illusory happiness of the people," that should be abolished as a condition for their true happiness. But the aban-
donment of illusions is not accomplished by means of an
intellectual activity. People cannot be persuaded to abandon their religious ideas. If people hold such ideas it is
because their situation demands it. It is necessary, then,
that their situation be changed, the wounds healed, in order that the illusions disappear.

> The demand to give up the illusions about its condition
> is the *demand to give up a condition which needs illu-
> sions*. . . .
>   Criticism has plucked the imaginary flowers from the
> chain not so that man will wear the chain without any
> fantasy or consolation but so that he will shake off the

chain and cull the living flower. The criticism of religion
disillusions man to make him think and act and shape
his reality like a man who has been disillusioned and has
come to reason. So that he will revolve round himself
and therefore round his true sun. Religion is only the
illusory sun which revolves round man as long as he
does not revolve round himself. [ibid.]

Marx foresaw the end of religion. It existed only in a
situation marked by alienation. When the alienation disappears, in a free society in which there are no oppressors,
whether they be capitalists, bureaucrats, or whoever
flaunts a sign of hierarchical superiority, then religion will
also disappear. Religion is the fruit of alienation. And
with this point the most devout religious people would also
agree. Building permits for temples are not issued in Paradise or in the Holy City.
 The error is to think that the sacred is only that which
bears traditional religious names. Durkheim aptly re-
minded us that the symbolical clothes of religion had been
changed. Wherever we conceive of values and add them to
reality, there is the discourse of desire, the exact place
where gods are born. And Marx speaks about a classless
society which no one ever saw, and a transparent vision
and crystal-clear insight into things, and the triumph
of liberty and the disappearance of oppressors and oppressed, while the State withers away from age and uselessness, while people play and laugh while they work,
planting gardens in the morning, building houses in the
afternoon, discussing art at night. . . . Indeed religious
symbols have disappeared, precisely those that were
"growing old or already dead." But I would ask myself if
the reason why Marxism was able to produce "hours of

creative effervescence, in the couple of which new ideas arose and new formulas were found which served for a while as a guide to humanity''—yes, I would ask myself whether this was due to the rigor of its science or to the passion of its vision. Was it due to the details of its explanation, or to promises and hopes to which it had given birth? And, if the latter were true, then, to the analysis which Marxism makes of religion as the opium of the people should be added another chapter about religion as the weapon of the oppressed, inasmuch as Marxism rightfully would have to be included as one of the weapons. It appears that the Marxist criticism of religion does not do away with it, but merely begins a new chapter. For, as Albert Camus correctly observes, Marx was the only one who understood that a religion that does not invoke transcendence should be called political (Camus: 196).

# CHAPTER SIX

# *The Voice of Desire*

*Religion is the dream of the human mind. [Feuerbach: xxxix]*

Indeed it is possible to view religion as if it were nothing more than discourse without meaning, as it was viewed by the empirical positivists. But, as Camus observed, it is not possible to ignore the fact that people find reasons to live and to die in their religious hopes, giving themselves to grandiose undertakings and daring to do wild deeds, composing poems and songs, marking the place where their beloved dead have been buried, and if necessary delivering themselves to martyrdom. Meanwhile, on the other hand, it seems that those proposing the liquidation of religious discourse have not yet produced their martyrs and can hardly offer reasons for living or for dying. I know that the comparison is unjust. But its purpose is merely to show that religious discourse contains something more than the pure absence of meaning. Precisely for this reason it cannot be exorcised by epistemological criticism.

On the other hand, it is also possible to analyze religion from a sociological angle, as did Marx and Durkheim. The same procedure can be applied to suicide. In fact, scientific analysis shows that the frequency and incidence of suicide follow, in a curious way, a certain social pattern: Protestants are more prone to commit suicide than Catholics, city-dwellers more than farmers, old people more than young, men more than women, bachelors more than marrieds. But however rigorous these analysis-results may be, we are left with a doubt: Can the explanation presented by the sociological charts tell us anything about *suicide*? Anything about that last night, when the decision was being made—the thoughts, the wringing hands? Who knows the prayers and the letters sketched out, the steps to the window, the sad eyes turned up to the tranquil sky? No, this drama-poetry that occurs in the solitude of the soul in its last deed is forever lost to sociological analysis. And, to be utterly honest, sociological analysis is absolutely indifferent to this drama.

If I mention suicide, it is to establish an analogy with religion. For in both cases sociological analysis maintains a total silence about what happens in the depths of the soul. If it is true that religion is a social fact, the person who makes promises to God that a child may live, or kneels in prayer, in solitude, weeping, or tastes the unutterable peace of communion with the sacred, or bows before the moral demands of faith, confessing sins that no one has known about and asking forgiveness of his or her enemy—this person (along with his or her religious sentiments) is, of course, situated in an area of experience which cannot be examined by sociological analysis because this area is intimate, subjective, existential. But does this make it less real?

And when we are ready to enter this sanctuary of subjectivity, we are again faced with an enigma. What are the reasons that lead people to construct the imaginary worlds of religion? Why do they not keep themselves within the stoical and modest realism of the animals which accept life as it is? These make neither songs, revolutions, nor religions, and thus escape the curse of neurosis and anguish.

And it was in the midst of thoughts like this that a religious person of the past century had a flash of vision that put religion in a totally different light.

Why not attempt to understand religion in the same way that we understand dreams? *Dreams are the religions of those who are asleep.* Religions are the dreams of those who are awake.

It is quite possible that religious people will feel disappointed, probably infuriated. What are dreams? Conglomerations of absurdities to which no one should pay attention. A phantasmagoric world of undefined contours in which things are and are not, in which we do things which we would never do if we were awake. And this is so true that frequently we do not have the courage to tell what we did in our sleep. Fortunately, we forget everything, almost always. And this is how the contemporaries of Ludwig Feuerbach thought also—those who condemned him to an intellectual ostracism for the rest of his life. It was too bold to say that religion is *only* a dream.

But if someone says "*only* a dream," that shows that they have not understood. Indeed, dreams do not correspond to the facts of life here on the outside. They are not the news of the day's events; of them it would be possible to say the same as was said for religious discourse: that they are without meaning, signifying nothing.

No one disagrees: oneiric symbols do not denote the external world. But, what if they were to be *expressions* of the human soul, symptoms of something that occurs inside us, revelations of our depths? This proposal could be accepted, except for the fact that none of us ourselves understand what dreams mean. Can it be that in our dreams we talk to ourselves in a language we don't understand? If our dreams are revelations of our inner beings, why is it that such revelations are not made in clear and direct language? Why the obscurity, the enigma?

Messages are written in code when there is someone who must not understand them. The code is a way to deceive the enemy. In that way the enemy will allow to pass through, as if harmless, the message that may mean destruction. And this is what seems to happen in dreams: we are the one who sends the message, and at the same time the one who must not be allowed to understand it.

This is exactly what psychoanalysis says.

We are split beings, tormented by an endless internal war, called neurosis, in which we are our own enemies. One of our sides lives in daylight, portraying legality and wearing the masks of an enormous theatrical company, playing roles recognized and respected by all—faithful husband, dedicated wife, competent professional, understanding father, wise and patient aged person—and, for the convincing portrayal, receiving the rewards of status, respect, power, and money. And everyone knows that breaking the laws that govern this world brings on punishment and leaves painful stigmas. Behind the mask, however, is another being—gagged, chained, repressed, beaten down, prohibited from doing or saying what it wants, without permission to see the sunlight, condemned to live in the shadows. This being is Desire, robbed of its rights and forcefully dominated by a strange, strong power: society. Desire screams, "I want to!" Society answers, "You may not," or "You must." *Desire seeks pleasure. Society proclaims order.*

And it is in this way that the conflict takes shape.

Society establishes prohibitions at those points where desire attempts to enter. It is not necessary to forbid people to eat rocks, because no one wants to. *Only the thing desired is prohibited.* Thus, there are laws prohibiting incest, theft, nude exhibitionism, sexual acts in public, cruelty to children and animals, assassination, homosexuality and lesbianism, and offenses against constituted authority. This is because such desires are very strong. The apparatus of repression and censure will be stronger in proportion to the intensity of the temptation to transgress the order established by society.

Everything would be simpler if repression were located outside of us and desire were housed within us. At least in that way the enemies would be clearly identified and separated. Meanwhile psychoanalysis affirms that, if it is true that the essence of society is the repression of the individual, the essence of the individual is the repression of oneself. We are the two sides in the battle—persecutor and persecuted, torturer and tortured. Is this not exactly what we experience in guilt feelings? We are our own accusers. And, in its most extreme form, this guilt leads to suicide: the person who commits suicide is at once executioner and victim.

We live in a permanent state of war with ourselves. We are unable to be happy. *We are not what we want to be.* What we want to be lies repressed. And it is precisely there, Feuerbach would say, that is to be found the essence of what we are. We are our desires—a desire that cannot develop. But, the worst of it all, as Freud observes, is that we are not even conscious of what we want. *We do not know what we want to be.* We do not know what we want, because our desire, repressed, has been forced to live in the regions of forgetfulness. It has become *unconscious.*

It so happens that desire is indestructible. And there, in the forgetfulness in which it is to be found, it does not stop sending coded messages—so that its captors cannot understand them. And they appear as neurotic symptoms, as lapses and equivocations, as dreams. *Dreams are the voice of desire*. And it is here that religion is born, as the message of desire, the expression of nostalgia, the hope of pleasure.

But the agreement between Freud and Feuerbach ends here. From here on they will travel in opposite directions.

Freud was convinced that our desires, however strong they might be, were condemned to failure. And this is because reality was not made to attend to the desires of the heart. The intension that we should be happy is not written into the plan of creation. Reality follows its stern way, in the midst of our weeping, and is deaf to it all. We get old, we get sick, we hurt, our bodies become flabby, beauty goes, the sexual organs do not respond to the stimuli of odor, sight, touch—and death moves inexorably closer. There is no desire that can alter the approach of the "reality principle."

In the midst of this hopeless situation, the imagination creates mechanisms of comfort and flight, by means of which people attempt to find, in fantasy, the pleasure which reality denies them. Obviously, these efforts are nothing more than illusions and narcotics, designed to make our daily life less miserable.

Religion is one of these mechanisms. Religions are illusions, fulfillments of the oldest, strongest, and most urgent desires of humanity. If religions are strong, it is because the desires they represent are. And what are these desires? Desires that are born from the need that people have to defend themselves from the crushingly superior power of nature. And we perceive that if we were able to visualize, in the midst of this cold and sinister reality that fills us with anxiety, a heart that feels and pulsates like ours—the problem would be resolved. God is this ficticious heart, which desire invented to make the universe human and friendly. And then death itself lost its threatening character. Religions are, thus, illusions which make life smoother. Narcotics. As Marx said: the opium of the people.

But they are condemned to disappear.

And this is because humanity follows a process of development quite similar to that through which each one of us passes. We are born as children and have the most pleasurable experience possible: the perfect union with the maternal breast. To grow up, however, we have to leave paradise, whose memory will never leave us. We have lost the breast and created substitute consolations: the thumb, the pacifier. But, the thumb and the pacifier are denied us also. And we seek to re-encounter the fulfillment of pleasure in toys, in which desire reigns supreme. But each step forward in maturity means a loss of artificial substitutes for pleasure. We are being educated for reality. We abandon our illusions. We leave the pleasures of fantasy. We adjust to the world. We become adults. In an analogous way, the beginning of the history of humanity is marked by the compulsion of pleasure. And people invented magical rituals and religious systems as expressions of the omnipotence of desire, in opposition to reality. Little by little, however, like a caterpillar leaving its cocoon, humanity has abandoned the illusions invented by the pleasure principle and crystallized in religion, to enter the adult world controlled by the principle of reality and explained by science. And in the same way that the development from infancy to adulthood is inevitable, the disappearance of religion is also inevitable—religion being a vestige, now definitively replaced by scientific knowledge, of an infantile moment in our history.

Is it not strange that Freud did not have the same sympathy for religion as he had for dreams? With respect to dreams he manifested a great care for details, endeavoring to interpret the most insignificant clues, because behind them the analyst could have access to the secrets of the unconscious. But with respect to religion, his judgment is all-encompassing and without any nuances. Religion is condemned as an illusion that must come to an end. The truth is that Freud was convinced that *desires are condemned* to failure, in view of the unalterable power of nature and of civilization. Hence the uselessness of dreaming. Dreams lead us to the past, to a paradise in which we had perfect and divine union with the maternal breast. But the past is over. And the future does not offer any possibilities for the satisfaction of desire. And that is the reason why men and women who are truly wise—scientists— voluntarily abandon desires, forget dreams, do away with religion. Desires must be repressed, whether voluntarily or by force.

For Freud, dreams are useless memories of a past which cannot be recovered. Feuerbach, on the contrary, sees in them flashes of the future. No, we do not want to say that dreams are endowed with prophetic powers to proclaim what has not yet occurred. Rather, for Feuerbach, dreams contain the greatest of all truths, the truth of the human heart, the truth of the essence of people.

Why is this essence portrayed in the enigmatic language of dreams?

Because the real conditions of our life impede and prevent their fulfillment.

But if this is factual, we have come to the conclusion that the human heart proclaims unceasingly, "What is, cannot be true." Just as the prisoner cries, "The bars cannot be eternal." Each dream is a protest, a denunciation, a refusal. If our desires for love can only be spoken in the dark nighttime chambers of locked rooms during the

hours of sleep and inaction, it is because public and political life, with their open spaces, and the clear, daylight
hours are the very opposite of desire. Reality is the nega-
tion of desire. Therefore reality should be abolished, in
order to be transformed. Freud concentrated on the uselessness of dreams. Feuerbach perceived that dreams are
confessions of secret and subversive projects; they are
statements, even though enigmatic, of utopias in which
reality will be harmonized with desire. And then every
human being will be happy. It is not surprising that in Orwell's book, *Nineteen Eighty-Four*, a man was sentenced
to prison for having dreamed. He had dreamed aloud. He
confessed that his own desires were far away and were
quite different. And without his even having known what
his heart desired (desires are unconscious!) he was put in
prison. And it is precisely about these desires that religion
speaks. And so it is that Feuerbach affirms:

> Religion [is] the solemn unveiling of a man's hidden
> treasures, the revelation of his intimate thoughts, the
> open confession of his love-secrets. [Feuerbach: 13]

We must stop here for a moment, to read, to re-read, to
meditate upon, to enjoy the poetic density of these words.
And he continues:

> Such as are a man's thoughts and dispositions, such is
> his God; so much worth as a man has, so much and no
> more has his God. Consciousness of God is self-
> consciousness, knowledge of God is self-knowledge.
> [Feuerbach: 12]

Thus, if psychoanalysis has said, "Tell me your dreams
and I shall decipher your secret," Feuerbach adds, "Tell
me about your God and I shall tell you who you are."

Man—this is the mystery of religion—projects his being
into objectivity, and then again makes himself an object
to this projected image of himself thus converted into a
subject. . . . God is the highest subjectivity of man. . . .
[ibid., pp. 29–31]

It is the human being who speaks, from the depths of his
or her being, in a language which even the speaker does
not understand. In spite of this, this human being always
speaks the truth, because he or she tells love-secrets and
proclaims to the world what can make it happy.

No, religious language is not a window, not a transparent glass, opening to the outside where other-worldly entities dwell. Religion is a dream. But in dreams we are not
in a void, as empiricism thought, nor in heaven, as the
theologians affirmed. Rather we are on earth, in the realm
of reality. What happens is that in dreams we see real
things in the magic splendor of imagination and fantasy,
instead of in the simple daylight of reality and necessity.
The sacred world is not a reality of the other side, but a
transfiguration of what exists on this side.

Here is dissolved the curse which empirical positivism
had cast upon religion. It had taken religious discourse as
if it were a window and, looking at the world outside,
asked: Where are the entities about which religion speaks?
Gods and demons? Sin and grace? Spirits? Astral influences? Nothing, absolutely nothing do we find corre-
sponding to these concepts. And Feuerbach laughed to
himself, as we laugh at those who compliment their own
images in the mirror.

The mirror. This is it: religious language is a mirror in
which is reflected that which we love most, our own essence. What religion affirms is the divinity of human beings, the sacred character of their values, the perfection of

their bodies, the goodness of living, to eat, to hear, to smell, to see. And in this way we arrive at the most surprising of the conclusions of this person who loved religion and in it found the revelation of the secrets of his own soul: The secret of religion, says Feuerbach, is atheism.

Necessarily! I shall only be able to recognize myself, in the image of the mirror, if I know that there is no one within it. I shall only be able to recognize myself in my ideas of God if I know there is no God at all, that I am the only absolute.

It is obvious that religious people cannot accept such a conclusion. And Feuerbach would conclude, because of this, that the meaning of religion is hidden from religious people. They dream, but do not understand their dream.

And thus religion is preserved as dream. The only problem is that, at the moment in which the dream is interpreted and understood, God disappears: *heaven* becomes *earth*, what was *up there* re-appears *out there ahead*, as the future. And the images that religion took to be portraits of the most beautiful and most perfect being are instead seen as constituting a horizon of hope on which people spread their desires, the utopia of a society in which the present is magically and miraculously metamorphosed by the person who breaks the chains to pluck the flower, not because of pressures from the outside, but in response to the dreams that come from inside. And everything is transformed before our eyes. For the religions, these kaleidoscopes of absurdities, are reshaped now as dream-symbols of the secrets of the soul, our own souls included. And behind the myths and rites, the ceremonies of magic and blessing, the processions and vows, we can perceive the contours, tenuous though they be, of those who await a new world, a new body. And their religious dreams are transformed into utopian pieces of a new order to be built.

# CHAPTER SEVEN

# *The God of the Oppressed*

*Mahatma Gandhi, Hindu leader, assassinated in 1948.*
*Martin Luther King, Protestant minister, assassinated*
  *in 1968.*
*Oscar Arnulfo Romero, Catholic archbishop, assassi-*
  *nated in 1980.*

Many centuries ago, long before the time of Christ,
there arose among the Hebrews a strange kind of religious
leader, the prophets. Who were they? Generally people
think that prophets are seers, endowed with special powers
to foresee the future, without much to say about the here
and now. Nothing is further from the work of the Hebrew
prophets—who dedicated themselves, with unparalleled
passion, to announcing and denouncing what was occurring in the present. So much so that their preaching was
closer to the political editorials of newspapers than to the
spiritual meditations of religious gurus. They did not con-
cern themselves much, if at all, with that which we popu-
larly consider to be the realm of the sacred: the cultivation
of mystical experiences, pious attitudes, and ceremonial
celebrations are practically absent from the scope of their
interests. Indeed, a good portion of their preaching was

taken up with attacking the religious practices prevailing in
their days, sponsored and celebrated by the priestly class.
And this is because they understood that the sacred, to
which they gave the name of the will of God, had funda-
mentally to do with *justice* and with *mercy*. In their
mouths such words had a political and social meaning that
everyone could understand. To understand what they were
saying one did not have to be a philosopher or theologian.
Their preaching was glued to the situation of the common
people. What was this situation?

The State was constantly growing, becoming more cen-
tralized and concentrated in the hands of a few. And, as
always happens when the power of some increases, the
power of others was diminishing. The small rural com-
munities, which in other periods had been the center of life
for the Hebrew people, had become weaker, due to the
heavy taxes which had fallen upon them. The weakness of
the people increased to the same degree that the power of
the armies grew—because without armies the State could
not survive. The farmers, in their poverty, had to sell their
lands, which were then transformed into large estates by a
small group of urban capitalists. It is from this kind of
situation that the prophets arose as the spokespersons for
the wretched of the earth. Everybody understood, therefore, when the prophets preached justice, that they were
demanding an end to oppressive actions. Life and happiness must be returned to the poor, the suffering, the weak,
the foreigners, the orphans and widows—in short, to all
those who found themselves outside the spheres of wealth
and power.

With the prophets a new type of religion was established, one of a political and ethical nature, and one that
understood that the relationship of humankind with God

had to demonstrate itself in the relationships of people
with each other:

> I hate, I despise your feast days. . . .
> But let judgment run down as waters. . . .
>                                   [Amos 5:21, 24]

The authorities, for obvious reasons, loathed the
prophets, accusing them of being traitors and denouncing
their preaching as contrary to the national interest. They
were prohibited from speaking, persecuted, and even
killed. And all the while they battled the power of the State
on one side, they faced the representatives of official religion on the other side. It became clear to the prophets that
the religion protected by the State had to be at its service.
Their prophetic denunciation, therefore, was directed not
only at those who had effectively oppressed the weak, but
also at those who had sacralized and justified the oppres-
sion, wrapping an aura of divine approval around it. And
thus it was that, twenty-five hundred years before anyone
had ever said that religion was the opium of the people, the
prophets perceived that even the names of God and the
sacred symbols could be used in the interests of oppres-
sion, and they accused the priests of being deceivers of the
people, and the false prophets of being preachers of illusions:

> Because, even because they have seduced my people,
> saying, Peace, and there was no peace; and one built up
> a wall, and, lo, others daubed it with untempered mor-
> tar. . . .[Ezekiel 13:10]

And in opposition to this false religion that sacralized
the present, they were weaving, of the pains, sorrows, and

hopes of the people, visions of an earth without evil, a utopia, a Kingdom of God, in which weapons would be transformed into plowshares, harmony with nature would be re-established, the dry and desert places would be changed into springs of water, the powerful would be dethroned, and the earth restored as an inheritance to the meek, the weak, the poor, and the oppressed.

It is probable that the prophets were the first to understand the ambivalence of religion: it could be used for opposite objectives. It all depended upon who manipulated the sacred symbols. It could be used to illuminate or to blind, to make one soar or to paralyze, to give courage or to make afraid, to liberate or to enslave. Hence the necessity of separating the God in whose name they spoke, who was the God of the oppressed, and who awakened hope and pointed toward a new future, from the idols of the oppressors, who made people fat, heavy, self-satisfied, rooted in their own injustice, and blind toward the divine judgment which was approaching.

But this lesson was forgotten. The memory of the God of the oppressed was lost. And it is not difficult to understand why. Visions similar to theirs had appeared only among the poor and the weak. But the poor and the weak go from defeat to defeat. Who would preserve their memories? Who would gather together their denunciations? Who would register their complaints? Such generosity on the part of the victors is not to be expected. It is the strong who write history, and this is the reason why one does not find written there the causes espoused by the defeated. Have you noticed how the defeated are always described as villains? What has remained, as history, has been the accounts which triumphant religion, hand in hand with the conquerors, has recorded of itself and of those who were crushed. And thus it is that, in our memory, there has remained only the religion of the strong, precisely those whom the prophets denounced. As for the religion of the prophets, it continues to emerge here and there. But those who grasped for the prophets' hopes were defeated. And for all practical purposes it was as if their religion had never existed. And the evidence thus appears to accumulate toward the conclusion that religion is nothing more than alienation, narcotic, illusion.

It was then that a series of coincidental factors permitted the reconstruction of the lost prophetic vision of religion as an instrument for the liberation of the oppressed.

First came the development of scientific history, which made possible the recovery of the fragments of the past, in an effort to penetrate beyond the curtain of interpretations which the victorious had erected. And there were found, frequently, revolutionaries who spoke in the name of God and in the name of the poor, regardless of whether they had a sword in their hand like Thomas Munzer, the Anabaptist, leader of the peasants in the sixteenth century, or whether they merely had the power of example and of nonviolence, as was the case with Saint Francis of Assisi.

Next came the development of the art of interpretation, which permitted us to catch a glimpse, between the lines of the speech of the victorious side, of the truth about those who had been defeated. The art of interpretation? For our purposes it is enough to know that "what Tony tells about Pete reveals more about Tony than about Pete." Thus, even though the losers have left behind few documents about themselves, in the very documents of the winners the truth has been hidden, as the negative of a photograph, as a complementary color, a kind of lining to the garment. What the oppressors have denounced in the oppressed is not the truth about the oppressed, but what the oppressors feared. Thus the official versions, justifying the massacre of the revolutionary movements of the peasants, describe the latter as fanatics, lunatics, and anarchists—thereby revealing the intensity with which the humble hoe-workers in the field questioned the domination of the oppressors. And the history of Brazil presents many examples of these movements, called messianic. Messianic? Yes. They hoped for a messiah, a representative of God, to exercise power and establish a just society upon the face of the earth.

At the same time, a new science called the sociology of knowledge was being worked out. Its beginning point is extremely simple: it notes that the way in which we think is conditioned by the social texture of our lives. One day I was having my shoes shined in a town square. The person shining my shoes saw someone else coming and commented, "Here comes another customer." I asked, "Somebody you know?" "No," was his reply. "Then how do you know that he is a customer?" To which he responded, "You didn't look at his shoes?" Thus it is that the eyes and thoughts of those who shine shoes follow the lines of their work. Their world is, we might say, divided between those who wear shoes and those who are barefoot. Those with shoes are classified as people who wear shoes that will take a shine, and those who wear sandals, tennis shoes, and suede shoes. . . . And so forth. Carried to its extreme, this line of thought would lead us to the conclusion that the powerful think differently from those who have no power: "The world of the happy is different from the world of the unhappy" (Wittgenstein:147).

But is it not true that every society has a dominant class and a dominated class? A class of people who can do what they want to and a class that cannot? A strong class and a

weak class? Even children and old people know this—
especially children and old people. Others who know it are
the migrants, the peasants devastated by drought, the sick
who die without medical attention. . . . And so forth. And
the conclusion that necessarily follows is that *the dreams
of the powerful have to be different from the dreams of
the oppressed. And also their religions.*

The powerful live in an oasis. Their power opens broad
avenues for their well-being, security, tranquillity, prosperity, profit, health. The future? The strong do not want
changes. Let the future be a continuation of the present.
And how do you perpetuate the present? First, by the use
of force. You build fortresses. Next it is necessary that the
dominators and the dominated accept the situation as le-
gitimate. Wealth by the will of God, poverty by the will of
God. Everything is covered by a sacred aura. But we already know that sacred things are untouchable. They demand reverence and submission, apart from any utilitarian
considerations. The sacred is destined for eternity, just as
is the world of power that it envelops. And this is why you
find flags in temples and why rituals of thanksgiving are
celebrated for the triumph of victors.

The situation is different for the dominated. They live
not in oases, but in deserts. Without power, without security, without tranquillity, from pillar to post, without
roots and without land, without houses, without work.
Their condition in life is one of humiliation. Sickness. Premature death. And the future? The weak demand change,
if not with their voices, because of fear, at least in their
dreams. Suffering prepares the soul for visions, says Buber. And it is in the poor and the oppressed that hopes
blossom—just as happened with the Hebrew prophets—
for a future in which they will inherit the earth.

Thus we find ourselves in the world of the prophets, in

which religion appears with all of its political ambivalence. The dreams of the powerful eternalize the present and exorcise a new future, while the dreams of the oppressed demand the dissolution of the present so that the future can be the fulfillment of the Kingdom of God, regardless of what name they give it.

It is ironic, but this conclusion scandalizes the Greeks as much as the Trojans. On one hand, those who were horrified at the statement of Marx that religion is the opium of the people are horrified now at the possibility that maybe it isn't. It would have been better if Marx had been right, because in that way those who hold power would not have to worry about the prophets and their hopes. But on the other hand, it is the Marxists themselves who cannot hide their perplexity. And this is because, in the eventuality that religions can revolutionize reality, the Marxists will have to admit that superstructural phantoms can become incarnate and make history.

A fascinating study of this subject is to be found in the article by Karl Mannheim entitled, "The Utopian Mentality," in which he analyzes the way in which desire and imagination impinge upon material factors to determine politics (Mannheim: 192–263). Quite unlike those who think that action is always the effect of an antecedent material cause, Mannheim suggests that what accurately characterizes politics, as a human activity, is the capacity that people have to imagine utopias and to organize their behavior as a tactic to realize them.
What are utopias? Realities? Not at all. As the name itself indicates, utopias refer to something not found anywhere (from the Greek *ou,* "no," and *topos,* "place"). How do they arise? Will they fall out of the air? No. They arise from the oppressed social classes which, not finding satisfaction for their desires in their *topos,* emigrate by

their imagination to a non-existent land where their aspirations will be realized. Their political activity becomes,
then, a pilgrimage in the direction of the Promised Land,
the construction of a world that does not yet exist.

That is what occurred with the Anabaptist peasants of
the sixteenth century. Moved by a profound religious fer-
vor, they began a revolutionary movement for the construction of a new social order in accordance with the will
of God. There were few who remembered them. Not even
Marx remembered these ancestors of the proletariat. An
understandable forgetfulness. The memory of the defeated
disappears easily.

But Engels did them justice. More than this, he believed
that he had found a similar ferment in the primitive Christian community. It is quite possible. Was not the Christian
community formed by groups destitute of power? And did
they not suffer every type of persecution? It is not surprising, then, that one of their sacred texts, Revelation, had
spoken about the hope of a total revolution in the cosmos,
in which all of the powers of evil, including the State,
would be destroyed.

But a problem remains, because this description that we
have made of the religion of the poor and oppressed does
not appear to correspond to reality. It is rare to see the
poor and oppressed involved with anything like the religion of the prophets. It seems that they feel more at ease in
the company of the magician, the healer, and the miracle-
worker, as they attempt to resolve their day-to-day problems without much hope, knowing that things are as they
are because of the unsearchable decrees of the will of
God—it being more certain that the poor will inherit
heaven than that they will inherit the earth.

And here we return to the sociology of knowledge. Is
there some alternative for those who experience daily im-

potence? Is it not their lack of power that leads them to push their hopes to another world? If this is true, what can you expect from a situation in which the poor and oppressed discover their power? It seems that when this happens they dare to transform their dreams into reality, making paradise come down from heaven to earth; having paradise on the horizon, they begin their march. And it is then that martyrs begin to appear. If religion were only opium, we would see the State and economic power on its side, protecting it as an ally.

But the martyrs have appeared: Gandhi, Martin Luther King, Oscar Romero, and many others. Religious leaders are arrested, persecuted, threatened, expelled, imprisoned. This would not happen if they were allied with power. They are witnesses to the political meaning of prophetic religion: the expression of the pains and the hopes of those who have no power. Opium of the people? Perhaps, but not here. In the midst of martyrs and prophets, God is the protest and the power of the oppressed.

# CHAPTER EIGHT

## *The Wager*

*On one side, the eternal star,*
*and on the other the uncertain wave,*
*my foot dancing upon*
*the edge of the seafoam,*
*and my hair upon a plain of desert light.*

*Silent I watch my days.*
*The more watched, the fewer!*
*With what sorrow I see the horizon . . .*
*near and without recourse.*
*What a pity, for life to be only this!*
*[Cecília Meireles]*

We have called and heard the witnesses: psychologists, philosophers, social scientists. Some, for the prosecution, have assured us that religion is a mad person babbling senseless things, handing out illusions, making alliances with the powerful, giving opium to the poor. Others, for the defense, have affirmed that without religion the human world could not exist, and that, when we decipher its symbols, we see ourselves as in a mirror. And further, that it is precisely with these symbols that the oppressed build their hopes and throw themselves into the battle.

It is strange, however, that none of the witnesses have ever been seen in the sacred places, seeking communion with the divine. And, what is more serious, it is a known fact that not one of them ever believed in what religion has to say.

That is how it is with scientists: they pay attention without believing. They listen and make notes, convinced that people do not know what they are talking about. They think that those who did not go through a scientific education, the common folk, are as sleepwalkers—walking enveloped in a cloud of illusions and ambiguities which do not allow them to see the truth. Nearsighted. Blind. Seeing things upside down. Not because of obstinacy, but because of a learning disability. And this is the reason why scientists hear their words with a condescending smile. Only scientists are able to distill from the conversation of common folk the truth to which only science has access. And this is why no scientist can believe in the words of religion. If he or she believed, he or she would be religious and not scientific.

No alternative remains for them. All the sciences, without exception, are committed to a *methodological atheism:* demons and gods may not be invoked to explain anything. Everything transpires, in science, as if God did not exist. And if it is from here that the scientists begin, how could they believe those who invoke gods and have the naïveté to pray?

But does not honesty impose a duty to hear from religion, which until now has been silent? Ought we not permit it to articulate its points of view? Or shall we conduct ourselves like inquisitors? In *Alice's Adventures in Won-*

*derland,* there occurred the famous trial in which the
Queen cried, "Sentence first—verdict afterwards" (Carroll: 147). Shall we follow the conduct of the mad queen?
No. We must hear the voice of religion, even if it is closer
to poetry than to science.

Whom shall I call as the witness for religion? You have
perceived that, in each chapter, I have forced myself to
assume the identity of the one in whose name I spoke. I
attempted to be a positivist; I attempted to be Durkheim; I
spoke as if I were Marx; as if I were Freud and Feuerbach;
I sought the visions of the world of the prophets. A strange
and marvelous capacity, to be able to play "make-
believe." To abandon our certainties in order to see how
the world looks from the viewpoint of another person.
And this is what we have to do now, requesting silence
from the scientist who lives in us in order to permit a different piece of ourselves to speak. A piece that, without
invoking the sacred names, insists on desiring, insists on
hoping, on sending up its silent cries of aspiration and
protest at the countless sinkholes of insomnia and suffering. We may not believe in gods, but we may well desire
that they did exist. This would tranquillize our hearts. We
should have certainties about the things that we love and
that we yet see, sadly, grow old, crumble, and disappear.
Ah, if we could but be pregnant with gods! This is how we
pass over to a world in which speech is not subordinated to
the eyes, but is connected to the heart. "The heart has its
reasons which are unknown to reason" (Pascal: no. 224,
p. 163).

An old sorcerer told his apprentice that the secret of his
art was in learning to make the world stop. Advice that
sounds like insanity, but that becomes wisdom when we
recognize that our world has been petrified by habit. We
become accustomed to talk about the world in a certain

way, we think of it always within the same framework, we always see everything in the same way, and feelings get dulled because they know that what is going to be is the same as that which already was. But when we play make-believe, it is as if our world suddenly stopped, to the extent that someone else's language, thought, eyes, and feelings make a new world arise before us. And this is what occurred to the poor frogs in this familiar parable, which I am going to repeat:

At a place not very far from here was a deep, dark well, where, from time immemorial, a community of frogs had lived. The well was so deep that none of them had ever visited the world outside. They were convinced that the universe was the size of their hole. There was more than enough scientific evidence to corroborate this theory, and only someone mad, destitute of sense and logic, would affirm the contrary. It happened, however, that a goldfinch flew by and saw the well, became curious, and resolved to investigate its depths. How surprised he was to discover the frogs! The latter were even more perplexed, because that strange feathered creature called in question all the age-old truths already grounded and proved in their society. The goldfinch could not have pitied them more. How could the frogs live imprisoned in that well without at least the hope of being able to get out? It is clear that the idea of leaving was absurd for them because, if their hole were the universe, there could not be an "out there." And the goldfinch started singing furiously. He trilled of the soft breeze, the green fields, the leafy trees, the crystalline rivers, butterflies, flowers, clouds, stars—which put frog society in a flurry and divided it. Some believed, and began to imagine how it would be out there. They

grew happier, and indeed lovelier. They croaked new
songs. The others frowned. Affirmations unconfirmed
by experience ought not to be worthy of our faith, they
alleged. The goldfinch had to be saying things that were
senseless lies. And they began to make their philosophical, sociological, and psychological criticism of its pre-
sentation. Whose cause was the goldfinch serving? The
dominant classes? The dominated classes? Was his song
a kind of narcotic? Was the bird crazy? Fraudulent?
Who knows if this might have even been a collective
hallucination? There was no doubt that the song had
created many problems. Neither the dominant frogs nor
the dominated frogs (who were secretly preparing a revolution) liked the ideas that the goldfinch was putting
into peoples' minds. Upon his next visit, the goldfinch
was imprisoned, accused of being a deceiver of the people, killed, stuffed, and all the frogs were forever prohibited from croaking the songs he had taught them.

This is what has happened: science has stuffed religion,
taking from it truths very different from those that religion itself sings. When religious people say sacred names,
they really believe in an "out there," and it is this invisible
world which their hopes feed upon. Everything is so distant and so different from scientific knowledge.

If we are to hear religious people, it will be necessary to
"make believe" that we believe them. Who knows? Maybe
the goldfinch is right. Who knows if it may be that the
universe is lovelier and more mysterious than the limits of
our well? What does religion talk about?

We must not allow ourselves to be confused by the ex-
uberance of symbols and gestures, from far and near,
from the past and the present, for the theme of the song is
always the same. Variations on a single theme. Religion

talks about the meaning of life. It says that life is worth living. That it is possible to be happy and smile. And what all religions propose is nothing more than a series of formulas for happiness. Here is to be found the reason why people continue to be fascinated by religion, despite all the criticism that science makes of it. Science has put us in a glacial and mechanical world, mathematically precise and technically manageable, but empty of human meaning and indifferent to our love. Max Weber said it well: The hard lesson that we have learned from science is that the meaning of life cannot be found at the end of a scientific analysis, however thorough it might be. And we find ourselves expelled from paradise, with the left-overs of the fruit of knowledge still in our hands.

The meaning of life: no question is formulated with more anguish, and it seems that everyone is haunted by it from time to time. Is life worth living? The seriousness of the question is shown by the seriousness of the answer. It is not rare to see people plunged into the abyss of insanity, or opting voluntarily for the abyss of suicide because they have received a negative answer. Other people, as Camus observed, are willing to die for ideas or illusions that give them reasons for living. Good reasons for living are also good reasons for dying.

But, what is this—the meaning of life?

The meaning of life is something that you experience emotionally without knowing how to explain it or justify it. It is not something that you construct, but something that occurs unexpectedly and without preparation, like a soft breeze that touches us without our knowing where it comes from or where it goes. We experience this meaning as an intensification of the will to live to the point of giving us the courage to die, if it were necessary, for the things that give our life meaning. It is a transformation of our vision of the world, in which things are integrated as in a melody. It makes us feel reconciled with the universe around us—possessed by an oceanic feeling, in the poetic expression of Romaine Rolland. It is an ineffable sensation of eternity and infinitude, of communion with something that transcends us, involves us and enwraps us, as if it were a maternal uterus of cosmic dimensions.

> To see a World in a Grain of Sand
> And a Heaven in a Wild Flower
> Hold Infinity in the palm of your hand
> And Eternity in an hour. . . .[Blake: 490]

The meaning of life is a feeling.

If religion's claim ended here, everything would be all right. For there are no laws that prohibit us from feeling whatever we want to feel. The scandal begins when religion dares to transform such a feeling, internal and subjective, into a *hypothesis about the universe.* We can understand the reasons why a religious person cannot be satisfied with the stuffed bird. Religion says, "The entire universe makes sense." To which science retorts, "Religious people *feel and think* that the entire universe makes sense." That sacred affirmation that echoes from universe to universe, reverberating in eternities and infinities, science imprisons within the small and dark well of subjectivity and of society: illusion, ideology. The meaning of life is destroyed. What can remain of the happiness of the frogs if the "out there" of which the goldfinch sang does not exist?

To affirm that life has meaning, and to propose the fantastic hypothesis that the universe vibrates with our feelings, suffers the pain of the tortured, cries the tears of the

abandoned, smiles with children who play. . . . Everything
is connected. The conviction that, behind everything visible, there is an invisible face that smiles, a friendly presence, arms that embrace, as in the famous canvas of
Salvador Dali. And it is this belief that explains the sacrifices offered on the altars and the prayers of those who
stammer in solitude.

It is possible that such images have never passed through
your head, and that you feel lost in the midst of the meta-
phors which religious experiences employ. I remember a
dialogue, one of the most beautiful and profound ever
produced by literature, in which Ivan Karamazov argues
with his brother, Alyosha, recalling the memory of a little
girl punished by her parents for having soiled the bed, and
locked in a small, dark, and cold room, outside the house,
on a frozen night. And he speaks of the little hands, beat-
ing her breast, asking to get out, tears rolling down her
face which was twisted by fear. What reasons, in the entire
universe, can be invoked to explain and justify such pain?
One senses that here is something profoundly wrong, eter-
nally wrong, always wrong, without attenuating circum-
stances, from the beginning of the world until its end. And
we feel the same way when we think of the tortured, the
executed, of those who have died of hunger, of the
enslaved, of those who lived out their days in concentra-
tion camps, of life destroyed by greed and reduced to the
level of the animal, of the weapons of war, of those abandoned in old age. And we could go on endlessly multiplying the examples.

What reasons do we bring with us that compel us to say
no to such acts? Could these reasons be our mere feelings?
But if this were true, what could we say when the executioner, the torturer, those who make the armaments and

wars also invoke their feelings as a guarantee of their actions? They also feel. They are still human beings.

No, our ethical judgments do not rest only upon our feelings. It is true that we rely on our feelings. But it is also true that we invoke the entire universe as a witness and guarantee of our cause. The voice of the heart vibrates with the infinite. We believe that the infinite possesses a human heart, a calling to love, a preference for happiness and liberty, just as we do. So, to announce that life has meaning is to proclaim that the universe is our brother. Our feelings are expressions of reality. And it is this reality, the anchor of feelings, that receives the name of God.

Religion, with special tenderness, has taken care to erect houses for gods and houses for the dead: temples and sepulchres. There is no other being in this world that, like us, raises supplications to heaven and buries its dead with symbols. And this is not accidental. Because death is that presence which, at one time or another, jabs us with its finger and asks, "In spite of me, do you still believe that life has meaning?"

How do you affirm the meaning of life in the face of death? What consolation can you give to a father whose son dies? Can you say that his life was short, but beautiful? How do you console the one who has learned that he has a fatal illness and sees the laughter and the loving moving away from him. And the millions who have died unjustly—Treblinka, Hiroshima, Biafra?

Everything is so different from a Mozart sonata—short, sweet. In twenty minutes everything that ought to have been said has been said. Nothing has interrupted the final harmony, it has concluded just as it should.

How do you affirm the meaning of life in view of the absurdity of existence as portrayed by the unfailing way death destroys what love has built and hoped for?

"What is finite to the understanding is nothing to the heart" (Feuerbach:6). This is the problem. "On one side, the eternal star, and on the other the uncertain wave . . ." (Cecília Meireles). The meaning of life is borne up on the meaning of death. And this is how religion delivers its dead to the gods, in hope. Between the houses of the gods and the houses of the dead shines the hope of life eternal, in order that human beings may be reconciled to death and liberated for life. When death is transformed into a friend, it is no longer necessary to fight against it. And is it not true that all of our life is a deaf battle to push back "indefinite and unmanageable" horizons. Society is a band of people who are moving along, fighting, in the direction of an inevitable death.

Think about what you would do if you were told you had only three months to live. After the initial panic, your daily routines, the things that you consider important, indispensable, for which you sacrifice your leisure, your meditation, your play, reading the papers, the checkstubs, the documents for Internal Revenue, the marital quarrels, the professional rancors, the graduate-study, the career-perspectives—all this would shrink away until it almost disappeared. And the present would gain a presence it never had before. To see and savor each moment because it is one of your last ones: the picture forgotten on the wall, the smell of jasmine, the song of a bird somewhere, the chirping of the crickets when sleep won't come, the yelling of children, the splashing of cold water near the fountain. Perhaps you might get up the courage to take off your shoes and wade in the water. Who would care if it shocked the solid citizens?

Perhaps we find here the reasons why society hides and dissimulates death, even making it a prohibited subject of conversation. The consciousness of death has the power to liberate, and this subverts loyalties, values, and the respect on which the social order depends. Putting the tombs into the hands of the gods, religion obliges the enemy to transform itself into a sister. Free to die, human beings become free to live.

But the meaning of life is not a fact. In a world still under the sign of death, in which the highest values are crucified and brutality triumphs, it is an illusion to proclaim harmony with the universe as a present reality. Thus the religious experience depends upon a future. It nourishes itself on utopian horizons that the eyes cannot see and that can be contemplated only by the magic of imagination. God and the meaning of life are absences, realities for which we yearn, gifts of hope. Indeed perhaps this is the great mark of religion: hope. And perhaps we can affirm with Ernst Bloch: "Where hope is there also is religion."

The vision is beautiful, but there are no certainties.

As the trapeze artist must leap out over the abyss, abandoning every point of support, the religious soul also has to leap out over the abyss, toward the evidence of feelings, of the voice of love, of the suggestions of hope. In the manner of Pascal and Kierkegaard, it is a matter of an impassioned wager. And what is thrown down upon the table of uncertainties and hopes is your entire life.

And the reader, perplexed, in search of a final certainty, asks, "But does God exist? Does life have meaning? Does the universe have a face? Is death my sister?" To which the religious soul could only reply: "I do not know. But I ardently *desire* that it be true. And I make the leap unreservedly. For it is more beautiful to risk on the side of hope than to have certainty on the side of a cold and senseless universe."

# Index

91